Macmillan Building and Surveying Series

List continued overleaf

List continued from previous page

Measurement of Building Services George P. Murray
1980 JCT Standard Form of Building Contract, third edition R. F. Fellows
Principles of Property Investment and Pricing, second edition W. D. Fraser
Project Management and Control David Day
Property Development: Appraisal and Finance David Isaac
Property Finance David Isaac
Property Investment David Isaac
Property Management: a Customer-Focused Approach Gordon Edington
Property Valuation Techniques David Isaac and Terry Steley
Public Works Engineering Ivor H. Seeley
Quality Assurance in Building Alan Griffith
Quantity Surveying Practice, second edition Ivor H. Seeley
Real Estate in Corporate Strategy Marion Weatherhead
Recreation Planning and Development Neil Ravenscroft
Resource Management for Construction M. R. Canter
Small Building Works Management Alan Griffith
Social Housing Management Martyn Pearl
Structural Detailing, second edition P. Newton
Sub-Contracting under the JCT Standard Forms of Building Contract Jennie Price
Urban Land Economics and Public Policy, fifth edition
    P. N. Balchin, G. H. Bull and J.L. Kieve
Value Management in Construction B. Norton and W. McElligott

Macmillan Building and Surveying Series
Series Standing Order
ISBN 0–333–71692–2 hardcover
ISBN 0–333–69333–7 paperback
(outside North America only)

You can receive future titles in this series as they are published by placing a
standing order. Please contact your bookseller or, in the case of difficulty, write
to us at the address below with your name and address, the title of the series
and the ISBN quoted above.

Customer Services Department, Macmillan Distribution Ltd
Houndmills, Basingstoke, Hampshire RG21 6XS, England

Auctioning
Real
Property

Richard M. Courtenay Lord

MACMILLAN

First published 1998 by
MACMILLAN PRESS LTD
Houndmills, Basingstoke, Hampshire RG21 6XS
and London
Companies and representatives
throughout the world

ISBN 0–333–68180–0

A catalogue record for this book is available
from the British Library.

This book is printed on paper suitable for recycling and
made from fully managed and sustained forest sources.

10   9   8   7   6   5   4   3   2   1
07   06   05   04   03   02   01   00   99   98

Printed in Great Britain by
Antony Rowe Ltd, Chippenham, Wiltshire

Contents

Preface

A colleague, when hearing that I had been invited to write this book, commented 'It is one thing to be an auctioneer and quite another to write about it.' How very true! The task has proved to be daunting, but I trust that I have faithfully attempted to record the 'best practice' of property auctioneers and, at the same time, not to have shied away from those contentious areas of our work.

As one who gained my rostrum skill in the time honoured way through acting as an auctioneer's clerk and understudy to the senior partners in my practice, I am the first to recognise that there is no substitute for 'hands-on' experience coupled with kindly guidance. Quite how our landed profession will ensure the education and training of future generations of auctioneers remains to be seen, but on the face of it this is an area which has largely been overlooked. Potential auctioneers are only able to gain a limited level of understanding and ability from diligent study of the subject, but in order to progress beyond that stage they require careful training, tuition and confidence building before conducting their first auction.

The book concentrates on the practical aspects of property auctioneering, and it is intended for students and those working in estate agency who are keen to gain an insight into the workings of this method of the transfer of property. In writing it I have drawn together all the threads of knowledge that have been passed down to me, together with my own experiences over 30 years on the rostrum, plus the considerable assistance and support of fellow auctioneers across the country. I have always believed that part of the benefit of belonging to a profession is the sharing of accumulated knowledge. In some small way I hope that this book is my remittance for the thoroughly enjoyable and satisfying working life which I have been privileged to enjoy as an auctioneer. I trust that others will be encouraged to follow!

As I mentioned, many have contributed in a variety of ways to this book. Owen Bevan of The College of Estate Management was the instigator, as he planted the idea in my mind, which in turn led to the late Professor Ivor Seeley who acted as my mentor, initial reader and guide. Malcolm Stewart at Macmillan coped with me as an unorthodox and inexperienced author and, no doubt at times, despaired of the book being completed. Those who read the draft copies and made so many valuable criticisms and suggestions include Richard Auterac of Jones Lang Wootton, Simon Riggall of Conrad Ritblat, Duncan Moir and Gary Murphy of Allsop & Co. and Charles Smailes of Feather Smailes & Scales. To those and many others I am indebted for their support and wisdom in drawing the book into its final form; without them it would never have gone beyond the initial draft!

1 Introduction

The origin of auctions reaches back into the ancient civilisations and almost certainly came about as a logical extension of barter. It is easy to imagine the scenario of a street trader in some bygone city faced with a throng of people anxious to buy his wares and chancing upon a crude form of auctioning the goods to the highest bidders. Soon others followed his example and gradually over the years disputes and arguments created a crude style and form of auction. From here it was but a small step to adapt the system for the sale of goods to anything for which there was a demand. The auction sale of real property as we know it today has been perfected and honed to its present form over many hundreds of years.

Early references to auction are sparse and the first known comment appears around 500 BC in *The Histories of Herodotus* where he writes about Babylonia. This record always causes amusement but it is fascinating because it demonstrates the full range of auction styles. Simply, Herodotus describes how each year a system was adopted to find husbands for the local girls. The auctioneer called the most attractive girl forward first and invited bids. In the early stages wealthy men bought attractive girls to become their wives. As the auction progressed a point was reached where the less attractive girls failed to draw bids, and so the role of the auctioneer switched to offering an incentive in the form of money or a dowry which increased as the increasingly less desirable girls were offered. This was financed out of the proceeds of sale on the earlier lots. From this first account of an auction it is clear that this method of sale was well established and had been refined over many years of common usage. The auctioneer not only conducted a sale with rising bids but also with descending bids, both of which are still found to be in use today: he also had a set of rules for resolving disputes which bound all parties to the transaction.

The Roman period saw the ascendancy of the auctioneer and references show them to be busy offering a wide range of commodities, property and even travelling with the armies to sell off the loot and captives of battle and conquest. The word auction stems from the Latin *auctio* which translates as increase. Interestingly, in the ruins of Pompeii a bust of an auctioneer, one Lucius Caecilius Jucundus, was found along with some of his wax tablet records. While every auctioneer has a high point in his or her career, usually a memorable or highly priced lot, one auctioneer alone holds the unique position of having sold a complete empire. This was in AD 193

1

The Incorporated Society of Valuers & Auctioneers, formed through a merger in 1968 of The Incorporated Society of Auctioneers & Landed Property Agents and The Valuers' Institution, is an important role player in promoting the interests of the property auctioneer. As with The Royal Institution of Chartered Surveyors, today entry is by examination and ongoing membership is monitored by participation in courses and lectures on a mandatory basis.

The National Association of Estate Agents is the third major role player and to date it has been primarily associated with traditional residential estate agency where its influence is substantial. However, relatively few of the members are active property auctioneers at present, although this may change in future years depending on circumstances which are discussed in Chapter 15.

Picking up the theme of the development of the role of the property auctioneer, major events over the years have influenced the pattern of business and the firms associated with it. While London became the natural centre for major property auctions, all provincial cities had active firms of estate agents and auctioneers, many tracing their origins to the early 1800s. Most country towns boasted a livestock market and sometimes alongside a produce market. These were important centres for the agricultural community and around them sprang up businesses supplying equipment and services. At main fishing ports similar markets were established concentrating on auctioning off the catches.

The First World War, followed by the traumatic period through to the Second World War saw the creation of new businesses both in London and the provinces, and with the established firms broadening their base to become truly general practices dealing with all the facets of urban and rural property to service the requirements of both the existing client base of landowners, and also a burgeoning merchant middle class. Usually a county firm would embrace agency, auctioneering of property, chattels and livestock, land agency and taxation.

After the Second World War general pratices initially continued in much the same style as in the pre-war years. Economic changes, the upheaval caused by the transition from the heavy manufacturing industrial base to the high technology production units, the advent of sophisticated computer and communications systems and the requirements of clients and society today, have all played a part in causing firms and the professional bodies to review their roles and place in a highly competitive market. These events are sufficient to fill a complete book alone, but suffice to say that the shape and form of the landed property profession has changed beyond belief. The role players and the emphasis of property auctioneers has to a large degree polarised into two camps: London and the major provincial cities. As always, there are exceptions and away from London in predominantly agriculturally based counties a few general practice firms continue to thrive.

2 The Property and the Vendor Client

The profession of the auctioneer is one which requires not only the exercise of skill on the rostrum but also the application of knowledge. An oft repeated old adage of working auctioneers is: 'You are only as good as your last auction.' How true!

A deep understanding of the property market and the relevant legislation is essential when bringing forward lots for auction and, once on the rostrum, the auctioneer must demonstrate clearly the ability to command the company of potential bidders, to respond to the unexpected, and to impart to the proceedings a strong sense of authority.

An overview of real property auctions today

From the multitude of instructions by vendors on any particular day across the United Kingdom the interesting fact is that only a minute percentage, probably as low as one per cent, will even involve a discussion as to the best method of sale. The majority of residential estate agents have no or at best only a passing knowledge of auctions and the presumption is to adopt automatically the private treaty sale route. When challenged for adopting this approach agents will counter either with the observation that their firm does not conduct auctions, or that they did consider this method but discarded it as inappropriate. In either case they failed to discuss with their the client the reasons for going down the private treaty road, rather than auction, or indeed tender.

While agents find no problem with this general approach to the lead-in for marketing property, there is the vital matter of 'best advice' and 'the duty of care' to be considered. Some would say that agents need to exercise more care at this early stage of the process when advising on the marketing, since sooner or later in these days of litigation and claims a disgruntled client is going to pursue an agent on these grounds. What then, one may ask, and how will the insurers react? These are interesting questions and no doubt in the way of the world today, sooner or later these issues will be aired in the courts. Meanwhile, agents will continue to advise on and market property with this open-ended question hanging over them unanswered; if they fail at the very least to make reference to the alternative route for disposal of real property, they proceed at their own risk. All methods of sale must always be examined in depth and the appropriate method, once chosen, must be explained to the client who in the light of the advice will make the decision as to which method to adopt.

These comments relate primarily to residential estate agents, rather than commercial, investment and industrial agents. Although most agents in many sectors of the commercial market can show signs of ignorance of the method, in

8

essence the ignorance stems from lack of knowledge and understanding of auction as a method of sale in many agency firms rather than its existence.

'*The Auction Professionals*'

On the instruction of
Enterprise Inns Plc
Sale by Auction of
25 Public House Properties
Wednesday, 20th December, 1995
commencing 2.00 p.m. in the Jubilee Suite
Grand Hotel, Colmore Row, Birmingham

Incorporating LEESON HACKETT Chartered Surveyors
Established 1846
Bigwood House 43a Calthorpe Road Birmingham B15 1TS
Fax 0121 456 4008

Telephone 0121 456 2200

Figure 2.1 Regional auction catalogue of a specialist sale
(Courtesy of Bigwood Chartered Surveyors)

Selecting suitable real properties for auction

A number of factors bear on the choice of an appropriate lot and the auctioneer must have at her or his finger tips a detailed knowledge of the current market. Major factors include supply and demand, both in the sector and in competing sectors, money supply and interest rates, prevailing yields, development potential, location and market confidence. These matters are expanded upon in detail subsequently.

As Gary Murphy, a partner of Allsop & Co, said in an address to a group of independent residential estate agents in 1996 'the traditional view is that a typical auction lot should firstly be difficult to value, secondly be of an unusual nature and thirdly be of anticipated wide market appeal. This remains fundamentally true and it is as good a test as any.' Part of the success of any market activity is in having two parties who hold differing views on value. An auctioneer's main task is to bring both parties together in an auction room, and to signify the successful conclusion of a transaction by the fall of the gavel.

In broad terms the categories of real property regularly seen in the auction rooms are:

Residential	**Commercial**
Homes	Retail investment property
Investment property	Industrial investment property
Ground rents	Office investment property
	Mixed use investment property
Agricultural	Licensed and leisure property
Landed estates	Ground rents
Farms	
Accommodation land	**Development land**
Sporting rights	Sites with planning consent
	Potential development sites

In all categories the lots may be freehold or leasehold, with the freeholds either with vacant possession or subject to leases or occasionally licences.

When selecting a lot for auction the question that always needs to be posed no matter what size, value, condition or type, is which method of sale will most effectively generate a sale at the best possible price, while at the same time fulfilling your vendor client's time frame and instructions. Auctions have the great benefit of bringing matters to a head

Ideally, for maximum impact it is preferable for the lot to be fresh to the market and not to have been offered by private treaty. However, there are important exceptions to this rule. The highly successful auction of large numbers of repossessed residential properties in recent years by London auction houses and regional auctioneers underlines this point. Similarly, investment and commercial lots together with development sites have all been successfully sold under the auctioneer's gavel at excellent prices recently, even though they had been on the market by private treaty beforehand.

Retail
Office
Commercial
Industrial
Investment

Broadly speaking these properties fall into three distinct groups. The first group consists of those lots that are prime sites and, if let, with blue chip covenants. Usually these do not come into the auction room because of vendor's resistance, limited timescale and the size/value of the lot. The agents handling the sales are able to place the properties quietly and without fuss. The challenge is whether or not the optimum sale price is achieved as it cannot be guaranteed when the lot has not been offered in the open market, preferably by auction. This is the nub of the debate on the merits of sales by auction as compared with private treaty. However, London auction houses are becoming increasingly adept in bringing forward lots from this first group into the auction room.

The second group is first class secondary property. This is by far the largest group coming under the hammer of the auctioneer. With commercial and investment lots this includes good parades of shops in popular secondary locations and where, if let, the majority of the covenants are held by well known retail traders. Likewise, the same criteria apply to office and industrial lots. The strength of the covenant and the cycle of rent reviews are important factors.

The third group is described by most auctioneers as the grey and uncertain lot. This includes the lesser secondary and tertiary property, perhaps with a preponderance of poor quality covenants or situated in a run-down or blighted district. This category is an important section and is frequently to be found in auction catalogues.

Another type of lot is one for which it is difficult to assess the market value for whatever reason. It includes those lots in poor, indifferent or awkward locations, and often with mixed occupations. When all is said and done, for many of these properties the challenge facing the agent is to determine what price a buyer will pay for the lot, rather than its true worth. This is an excellent reason for going to auction.

Residential

In this section the majority of buyers are owner occupiers. Again there are basically four distinct groups here. The first group is property for renovation; the more run down the better! Whether it is a terraced unit, a detached country cottage or a former vandalised Edwardian mansion, this type of lot will generally attract plenty of interest from bidders, not only for owner occupation but also from builders, developers and speculators.

The second group consists of country homes, often with a good sized plot or a few acres of adjoining land, and those of character. These range from the listed village house or cottage to the old rectory. The land element may just be a large garden, a 'pony paddock', or an actual or potential building plot.

Into the third group fall those lots which are best described as 'plain unusual'. Examples include lock keepers' cottages, windmills, former railway stations and old water towers; the list is endless.

The make-up of the fourth group is extremely flexible and to a large degree is dictated by current market conditions. For example, at the height of the property boom in the late 1980s developers were able to sell homes on residential housing developments off the plan before they were built! To wind up an executor's estate of an ordinary town house, auction rather than private treaty might be the preferred route, but a year later the same advice might not be appropriate. Supply and demand together with the requirements and background of the client are key factors in reaching a decision.

Another element in this category is the property with potential or actual planning consent for a change of use, perhaps from residential to hotel, office use or retirement home.

Typical lots today include mixed residential and retail or office properties; for example tertiary shops with flats above.

Development and Potential Development Sites

A familiar lot in the auction room is the small parcel or single plot of building land for residential development.

Larger parcels of land and complicated sites, sometimes in multiple owner-ship, are not unknown but more unusual.

Landed Estates, Farms and Accommodation Land

The range and diversity of lots in this section is very broad and often involves the auctioneer in the fascinating art of lotting for sale.

At one end of the spectrum is the large landed estate including several thousand acres, perhaps with one or two farms tenanted and the remainder of the land in hand, cottages (usually let), a public house, village shop, the principal residence, woodland, and sporting rights. At the other end are a few acres of accommodation land, usually referred to as a pony paddock on the edge of a village.

Interestingly, outside the major collective auction sales in London and a few major provincial cities, farms and agricultural properties constitute an important and enduring element of the auction scene in the provinces and to this day they are usually sold locally.

NINETEEN DAYS' SALE AT STOWE

By direction of the Right Hon. The Baroness Kinloss, C.I.
The Rev. The Hon. L. C. F. T. Morgan-Grenville, Master of Kinloss, and the Trustees of the will of the late Duke of Buckingham and Chandos, G.C.S.I.

THE DUCAL ESTATE OF STOWE
NEAR BUCKINGHAM.

The Historical Seat of the Dukes of Buckingham and Chandos
and for some years the residence of the late Comte de Paris.

MESSRS. JACKSON STOPS

WILL SELL BY AUCTION, AT STOWE HOUSE,

On Monday, July 4th, 1921, at 1 o'clock
THE FREEHOLD OF THE HISTORIC

MANSION & ESTATE

Extending to about 1,400 acres, including the World-famous Grounds, and Temples, Surrounding Park Lands, and the Picturesque Village of Dadford,

The Estate will be first offered as a whole, and, if not then sold, in 67 lots, including 24 First Pasture Farms and Small Holdings, chiefly with vacant possession; Houses and Freehold Ground Rents, at or near the Town of Buckingham.

On the eighteen days following (from July 5th to July 28th excluding Saturdays, at 11 o'clock precisely each day) will be sold the

Contents of the Mansion

Including the Supremely Valuable Collection of

Heirloom Pictures, Tapestries and Historic Furniture, by the World's Greatest Masters, Superb Statuary and Metal Work, important collection of Rare China, Porcelain, an immense assortment of other Objets d'Art, the Contents of the Magnificent Library, fine collection of Historic Letters and Manuscripts, the Valuable Gold Plate, Carvings and Panellings by Grinling Gibbons,

FAMOUS CLASSIC TEMPLES
and other Buildings and Bridges luxuriously
built to designs by famous architects.

Finely Illustrated Catalogues, with Historical Preface, Plans and Particulars (which will admit three persons to sale) price 25/- may be obtained from

MESSRS. JACKSON STOPS, F.S.I., F.A.I., Northampton and Towcester.
MESSRS. SMALL & BARKER, Solicitors, Buckingham.
MESSRS. WITHERS, BENSONS CURRIE WILLIAMS & CO., Solicitors, Howard House, 4, Arundel Street, Strand, London, W.C. 2.
JUDGE PATTERSON, City Hall, Philadelphia, U.S.A.

Figure 2.2 1921 auction catalogue for a 10 day sale of the Stowe Estate by Messrs Jackson Stopps

Sporting Rights

Fishing rights are the most common type of lot sold under this heading. In all instances the background to the title and leases needs to be examined with great care, especially where the title of the land has been separated from the ownership of the fishing rights by virtue of an earlier sale. Sometimes the land was sold and the original owner continued to exercise the fishing rights for many years. In this instance the position must be checked to avoid any uncomfortable questions being raised in the auction room.

Other examples include grouse and pheasant shooting rights from a single gun up to the entire rights of a specified area. Moorings and boating rights including either the freehold or leasehold of the river bank have occasionally been sold by auction.

Ground Rents

Many will not be familiar with this type of ownership where often property was built and sold on 99 or 999 year leases. Traditionally these were commonly found in a few major provincial cities and in London. Developers reintroduced the Ground Rent in the 1980s during times of rapidly rising land values as a means of holding down the sale price of the completed homes.

Today the supply of blocks of Ground Rents coming forward for sale is in diminishing supply and demand from investors and dealers looking forward to selling the freehold to the lessees is keen.

Licensed and Leisure Property

The licensed and leisure sector has made use of the auction route for centuries with it being common practice to sell the public house or hotel at the property auction in times past. During the 1980s recession many bingo halls, former theatres and cinemas that were usually housed in large buildings where alternatives uses were hard to identify, began to appear in the auction room. Here the benefits of extensive marketing and sensible price guides ensured active bidding resulting in sales of lots which were sometimes virtually impossible to value. In early 1987 Conrad Ritblat successfully auctioned a 40 lot catalogue of surplus theatre and cinema properties with all sold under the gavel. They followed on a few months later with a larger catalogue of similar lots including bingo halls and so paved the way for multi-lot auctions as an established route for the sale of leisure property.

In the licensed trade sector the change in circumstances as a result of the 1989 Monopoly and Mergers Commission Investigation led to an urgent need to identify public houses that were performing badly. As an example from the early 1990s Conrad Ritblat started entire catalogues devoted to public houses owned by one or two breweries. The result was an immediate broadening of the ownership base. However, until the mid 1990s there was practically no institutional investment market for this sector, but with the introduction of landlord and tenant rights and 'Institutional Lease' a new market has emerged with institutional and property company buyers willing to invest significant sums in public house investments.

Auctions and insolvency

The effects of the property recession during the early part of the 1990s saw many hundreds of thousands of properties being repossessed by the banking sector. Many of the properties were the subject of excessive loans based on valuations adopting rather optimistic views on the future growth potential. With the closure of many companies, this led to countless tenants becoming insolvent, including major multiples in the retail sector. This was heightened by the effect of the growth of out-of-town retail parks that reduced the demand for the traditional town centre property.

Auction was seen as an excellent route for disposal, providing high profile marketing and the capability of handling a large number of lots in a single sale. Both clients and the auctioneers faced difficulty in setting realistic reserves, especially as many vendors had to meet substantial losses on sales.

Auctions in the public sector

Following the capping of public sector spending by the last Conservative government, local authorities in particular had to review their assets and dispose of those which had no relevant operational value and to cost the use of all property held in their portfolios. With each department, such as nursing homes, schools and offices facing notional rents on their properties, extensive closures and rationalisation of assets followed. Many local authorities chose auction as the method of disposal, especially as they were required to achieve the optimum value coupled with full exposure to the market place.

As an indication of this market, Simon Riggall of Conrad Ritblat reports that in 1996-8 his firm disposed of more than £50 million worth of public sector property by auction. He observes that many urban councils own their town centres and have become significant players in the investment market with the disposal of not only surplus property, but also investment lots previously held for rental purposes. Looking ahead he anticipates that other significant role players include the Ministry of Defence and Health Authorities that have been criticised for their slow rate of disposal from their enormous surplus assets when the Government is looking to them to provide funds.

Understanding your client's requirements

As with so many activities in the property world the auction file starts life with the all important and dominating element – the client. For the auctioneer the fundamental rule is to know and understand your clients in depth, the timescale within which they are working, their financial constraints, and their objective in selling. Many factors will bear on the decision to dispose of a property and they must be grasped and clearly understood from the outset.

Where you are not acting for an individual living owner or lessee, then the first challenge is to establish the chain of command of your corporate, institutional, or trustee client. The types of client that will commonly be met in the course of auction work include:

- Multinational companies
- National companies
- Provincial companies
- Private companies
- Banks and Building Societies
- Pension and Investment funds
- Government Bodies including HM Armed Forces
- Local Authorities
- Statutory Authorities,

- Trustees and Executors
- Liquidators and Receivers
- Ecclesiastical Bodies
- Crown Commissioners
- Trusts

By their very nature company structures are often complicated and each internal subsidiary or department will jealously guard its area of responsibility. For example a service group subsidiary looking after property with a broad remit covering maintenance, improvements, tenure, acquisitions and disposals may have to report through a series of boards up to the main holding board when sales off are involved. This process can not only be time consuming, especially when arranging a collective auction, but also frustrating to all parties concerned.

A similar situation may be encountered with local and statutory authorities and Government departments. With banks and lending institutions the initial question that arises is 'Who is the vendor?', as the sale might be through the authority of a court or as an executor or trustee.

The route by which the instructions or invitation to act on a sale will come range through a variety of sources from a solicitor or accountant to the chairman or an employee of the client company.

As a first step the auctioneer must establish the lines of communication and, equally vital, the decision making procedures. For example, if one is meeting and corresponding with the head of the Property Department, then it is essential to know the process and timing of the client company in reaching authoritative decisions on such matters as the reserve price. Sometimes there will be delegated authority once the basic decision to go to auction has been made, but in others it may be necessary to allow plenty of time for reference to meetings of Committees or Boards who perhaps only meet on a pre-scheduled monthly or occasional basis.

It should be recalled that with an auction, unlike a private treaty sale, the time clock is running from the moment confirmation of the instruction to proceed to auction is received from the client. To find out too late that it will take two weeks to obtain a decision on an offer prior to the auction date, or that a decision on your recommendation on the reserve price cannot be made in time for the auction sale date, can cause more than a small degree of embarrassment and extreme annoyance to all concerned!

It is essential that the auctioneer provides a clear and concise written brief to the client setting out the basis of the instructions, the authority and to whom correspondence, reporting and enquiries must be addressed. This must be in writing and not verbal. A few simple questions and gentle probing with the person representing your vendor client at the initial meeting will avoid a great deal of grief and frustration at a later stage by establishing the chain of command at the outset.

The key questions which need to be constantly in the mind of the agent are:

(a) Will there be competition for the lot?

(b) How does the expectation of the realisation price by the vendor client relate to the market price?

(c) Is there a known special purchaser, perhaps an adjoining owner?

(d) Is the property unique in some way?

(e) Is the lot a property which for some reason is difficult or nigh on impossible to value?

(f) Is the client a trustee, receiver, executor or mortgagee in possession? Where there is a financial interest auction may be the preferred route.

(g) What are the requirements and the timescale of your client to achieve a sale?

These are the main questions and issues which face the agent and the client, and the answers in part will determine whether or not to opt for an auction as opposed to a private treaty or tender as the method of sale.

Advantages of an auction – From all points of view

1. Openness and lack of bias

By virtue of its nature auction is an 'open' process. This eliminates any question of deals behind closed doors, gazumping and the like. Everyone interested can attend the auction sale and bid according to their wishes, subject only to their personal financial constraints. If they fail to purchase it is because someone outbid them in the room, or because the seller placed a reserve at a level above the bidding. Where there are indications of strong demand for a lot, or special buyers with vested interests, or concerns on the part of the seller, who may be acting in the role of Executor or Trustee, then an auction has many attractions. Fair play and a lack of bias towards any one party are key elements in choosing an auction as the preferred method of sale.

2. Certainty and immediacy

Auction is extremely effective as for all parties there is certainty and immediacy. The lot is described clearly in the particulars; the Conditions of Sale and other legal documents are available; there is usually a price guide; often a survey or House Buyer's Report is available; the sale date and the completion date are stated. There is no variation of any of these facts as between one bidder and another, and the vendor, so all parties come to the auction on equal terms. The result for the successful bidder is immediate and for both parties to the transaction there is no room for doubt or uncertainty.

3. Known timescale for exchange of contracts and completion

The timescale of an auction determines not only the sale date but also the completion date. Everyone knows exactly where they stand. This can be an attraction to both the vendor and the purchaser.

Advantages of an auction – From the vendor's point of view

1. Establish the true open market value

The auction sale brings together all the able bidders on the sale day and establishes the best price at that moment in time. As the bidders are able to compete openly and without rancour in the sale room on a level playing field the person who is prepared to go to the highest price, at or above the reserve, will be the successful buyer.

2. Binding contract achieved at the auction

On the fall of the hammer a binding contract is made with a known time gap to completion. Unlike private treaty there is no negotiation over the Conditions of Sale and Contract, nor over price reductions as a result of a surveyor's report, mortgage offer, or problems down the chain. Bids are made unconditionally and are therefore 'subject to nothing'.

In a single word there is 'certainty'.

3. Opportunity to achieve a premium price

Competition in the auction room can lead to a premium price being paid. The fact is that each person bidding for a lot will have individual criteria dictating the upper limit of their final bid. This is usually a combination of the depth of their pocket and their desire to secure the property. For example an adjoining owner is likely to be able to outbid other parties because the marriage value of the two holdings is probably going to give greater flexibility for the final bid. This is particularly the case where the original site has been owned for some years, or an overall site area enables a more valuable planning consent to be obtained on the combined property.

4. Maximum exposure in tight timescale to the market

The nature of an auction sale ensures that the marketing is concentrated into a tight timescale ranging from 4 to 12 weeks, depending upon the type of lot. Through the various specialist publications, such as the *Estates Gazette* on a national basis, and local provincial papers which often carry special auction sections, the auctioneer can ensure that the optimum number of interested bidders is reached.

This is in addition to the use of the mailing list which for a major London collective sale will involve mailing around 12,000 applicants and regular subscribers.

5. Prompt decision making by bidders

Again by virtue of the timescale both seller and would-be buyers are forced into making decisions promptly. There is no room for prevarication.

6. Imposition of clauses and covenants by vendor

For the vendor when selling off an adjoining building plot, cottage, or farmhouse yet retaining surrounding property, an attraction of auction is the ability to impose covenants on the lot which are not open to variation, as is so often the case in private treaty sales. Negotiations on the terms and conditions of the Contract and Special Conditions of Sale, so familiar in private treaty sales, do not apply. Potential bidders have to decide whether or not they are prepared to bid on the stated terms.

Examples include the use of the lot, approval of plans for external alterations, rights of access and connection to services, such as drainage, and design and materials of boundaries.

180 Lots
For Occupation, Refurbishment, Investment and Development

For Sale by Auction
(unless previously sold or withdrawn)

By Order of

Halifax plc   HALIFAX

Woolwich plc   WOOLWICH

British Telecommunications plc   BT

The Receiver for The Metropolitan Police District

The London Borough of Redbridge   Redbridge

The London Borough of Haringey   HARINGEY COUNCIL

The London Borough of Hackney   Hackney

London & Quadrant Housing Trust

Rhondda Housing Association Limited   Rhondda

London and Continental Stations & Property Ltd

Grainger Trust plc

Mountview Estates plc

Liquidators, Mortgagees, Receivers, Trustees, Executors, Public and Private Property Companies and others

To be held on
Tuesday 10th February 1998
at
The May Fair Intercontinental, Stratton Street,
London W1
Morning Session: Commencing at 10.30 a.m. precisely
Afternoon Session: Commencing at 2.00 p.m. precisely

0171 494 3686
100 Knightsbridge
London SW1X 7LB

Catalogue request line:
0115 972 6222

Figure 2.3   180 Lot Collective Sale
(Courtesy of Allsop & Co)

Advantages of an auction – From the agent's point of view

1. The opportunity to establish a niche market
Auctions offer agents the chance to establish a niche market and so expand their business base and fee income.

2. The ability to secure payment of commission and expenses
By virtue of the letter of appointment and the agreement with the vendor client, the auctioneer establishes the exact parameters within which the liability and circumstances for the payment of commission and expenses arises out of an auction.

3. Achieve appointment as the Sole Agent
The auctioneer always acts either as Sole or Joint Sole agent and this gives greater control over the marketing of the lot and a closer relationship with the vendor client.

4. Generation of additional applicant traffic
The process of auction brings a whole range of new applicants in touch with the agent.

Hopefully, an auction lot will create additional visitors and enquiries to the agent's office, giving fresh opportunities to enlarge both the applicants' register and the property register. As there is only one successful buyer, one or two underbidders may leave their homes on the market with the auctioneer, having made the decision to move home, and the applicants' register will be increased with a useful number of genuine enquiries.

Disadvantages of an auction – From the vendor's point of view

1. The costs
There can be additional costs as compared with a private treaty sale. This applies not only to the vendor but also the bidders. A fact frequently overlooked is that anyone considering bidding at auction is likely to have incurred professional fees in seeking advice and guidance from solicitors, surveyors, specialists, and financial advisers.

Regional variations reveal as a broad statement that agents in the north of England charge extra for advertising and other marketing expenses, both for private treaty and auction sales. In the south of England for residential sales the commission charge is often inclusive of the other marketing expenses. Again the picture is confused by the variations as between multi-agency and sole-agency appointments.

For collective sales there is often a fixed catalogue entry charge geared to a whole, half or quarter page insertion, inclusive of advertising and promotion costs. Commission on the sale price is the subject of separate arrangements between the vendor and the agent.

2. The sale price is public knowledge
The fact that the auction will be in the public domain and the sale price will be public knowledge. Not only some purchasers, but also some vendors, prefer their

deals to remain totally confidential. This is not considered to be an issue of any consequence by auctioneers, but it is one that is quoted as an adverse factor occasionally.

3. Blighting a property by an abortive auction
An abortive auction if handled poorly could place a stigma on the lot and depress the eventual sale price.

4. Exclusion of potential bidders
Some bidders for residential property with possession will be prevented from coming to the auction. Perhaps they have not obtained an exchanged contract on their present property, or they have insufficient funds to pay for the pre-auction enquiries of solicitors, building society, and surveyors, or simply they will not attend an auction for whatever reason.

5. Inability of the vendor to choose the purchaser
The vendor does not have the opportunity to select the purchaser.

6. Presentation of the property
With owner-occupied residential property the need to maintain good presentation during the marketing period is regarded by some as a disadvantage.

7. If unsold, the sense of failure
While the vendor will often feel dismayed if their lot fails to sell under the hammer, the proven fact is that generally lots will either sell in the room immediately after the auction or a few days later.

Disadvantages of an auction – From the agent's point of view

1. Working to a tight timescale
By the very nature of an auction the whole office must maintain the time schedule leading up to the auction date, and all the staff, from front-line receptionist to the auctioneer, need to be aware of and convey the urgency to applicants, interested parties, and the client.

2. The 'hassle' factor
Viewings and queries to be sorted out will be concentrated into a shorter period as compared with a private treaty sale.

For viewings of residential properties the use of 'open home' days can help to take the pressure off the auctioneer and the vendor. There is also the added benefit of underscoring to the applicants the strength of interest when several families are looking over a property simultaneously.

3 The Initial Steps

The source of instructions will arise in various ways, the most common being through personal contact with your client or their advisors. A frequent comment from many seasoned auctioneers is that their clients have often not even considered auction as a possible method of sale. At this stage the agent will be well advised to suggest the possibility of an auction to the client as a possible method of sale, and to develop this theme once the property has been inspected.

The instructions

Basic common sense and normal business courtesy demand that an acknowledgement by letter or fax is sent on the same day of the receipt of instructions and also that an appointment is made to meet your client and/or inspect the property as soon as possible. Another practical tip is always to read your instructions at least twice. If they are given to you verbally, then make a written note on file of what was said, and again write to your client contact setting out what was said. In the present day business climate the agent must record faithfully for his/her own protection a fully annotated written note of all that was said and discussed on the file. Refer to the subsequent section in this chapter 'The auctioneer's terms of engagement'.

The normal procedure is for agency contracts to be sent out to the clients as soon as possible in order to avoid the situation arising where, if they are dispatched at a later date, they may not be enforceable. If there is a delay, there is always the possibility that the discussions will have created the framework of an agreement between the client and the principal, the auctioneer. In any event the agent is required by the Estate Agents Act 1979 to give the client written confirmation of the fees, expenses and business terms before that client is committed or has any liability towards the agent. This requirement is reinforced by the codes of conduct of the main professional organisations representing qualified agents.

Market research and the market place

Essential to the business of any successful agent is a detailed and up-to-date knowledge and understanding of both the geographical area in which that firm operates, and the wide range of factors which relate to the particular area of activity. The agent must have an up-to-the-minute personal grasp of what the market is doing – sales, purchases, and leases – and the length of time taken to conclude them. He or she should also know who is active and who is about to enter or leave the market.

Other factors include the national, international, as well as the local political scene, which may have a direct bearing in so many ways on the level at which deals are closed.

Resulting from our membership of the European Union and dependent upon the philosophy of the political party in government, a wide range of issues will affect the level of value and demand for particular types of property. In some parts of the country inward investment will be actively encouraged, either driven by policy from Brussels or London and with grant aid on offer from European, central and local government. Major international manufacturers may be attracted to the United Kingdom not only for these reasons but also for ease of access to the European market, good labour relations, and the wealth of inventive talent for which this country is renowned.

The constraints of planning are subject to major changes in direction and policy which directly relate to the government of the time. Current issues include transport, development in Green Belts and the creation of major new urban schemes on green field sites.

Remember also that movement in interest rates, the money supply, regional aid and grants, together with the level of local taxes are all factors to be encompassed in the equation.

Only when armed with the full facts can the agent discuss authoritatively with the vendor client the property in question and the appropriate method of sale. Simply expressed, the agent must be streetwise!

The initial inspection

Always allow plenty of time for your first inspection. Take with you an extract of the large scale Ordnance Survey sheet and a street map of the area. Before going to the property drive around the district, familiarising yourself with the neighbourhood and how it works. Look out for obvious indicators such as empty property, agents' signs, new building, major employers and existing developments in the district.

A camera is a useful tool, because after shooting off a roll of film the photographs provide an excellent *aide-mémoire*, jogging the memory on the layout, condition, adjoining properties and the like.

Always include in your site inspection file comparisons of similar lots which have been sold recently, preferably taking copies of particulars, and any appropriate Structure and Road Plans. Armed with this type of background information the agent will be better able to show clearly and authoritatively to the client his or her grasp of the task ahead.

The need to establish at this meeting the chain of command for decision making has already been discussed. This essential point should be clarified at the earliest possible moment.

However the meeting is conducted, full detailed file notes must be recorded. Use the opportunity of the meeting to walk the boundaries, comparing them with any plans or other detail that has been provided in advance. Be on the lookout for infringements, areas of uncertainty, easements and rights of way.

Plans, conveyances, leases, planning and building regulation consents are only some of a vast range of documents relating to property ownership and occupation which may be made available. List them in detail and whenever possible borrow them to make file photocopies, taking care to return the originals promptly.

When referencing the property always work in accordance with The Royal Institution of Chartered Surveyors' and The Incorporated Society of Valuers & Auctioneers' current edition of *The Code of Measuring Practice*. This is your defence in the event of someone taking issue over measure-ments. Accuracy and the correct representation of all measurements is essential.

In summary, an extra hour spent at this stage can save endless heartache and wasted time and expense at a later stage once the auction is rolling. Imagine that the lot is in a multi-lot catalogue which has been mailed out to 9000 addresses and then an error is discovered. The cost of sending out an addenda alone is substantial!

The initial discussion

In the forefront of your mind keep firmly implanted your duty of care and best advice which, as the agent, you owe to your client. Always listen carefully to all that is said, note down all points, and take your time to get to the root of all the issues which your client and yourself feel are pertinent. Use the meeting as your golden opportunity to gain as much background information as possible.

Simple pointers as to why a decision has been made to sell, the financial background, the timescale, and the personalities involved are all essential elements in the advice which the agent will give.

It may come as no surprise that many clients, corporate and multinational groups included, have little or no understanding of auctions and how they work. Use the meeting to explain the auction system and ideally leave your brochure on the subject along with any other background material on your firm.

An important factor to draw out at this meeting is the realisation figure which your client is seeking. This figure, once established, will be a strong pointer as to whether or not your client will be inclined towards an auction, all other factors being favourable. Given an over-optimistic figure and an intransigent attitude on the part of the client an auction will probably be a non-starter because the Price Guide and its relationship to the Reserve, as discussed in later chapters, will result in a figure being quoted ahead of the perceived market value. If it is known to the auctioneer from the outset that the reserve will be set at a given level, then the Price Guide must be stated within the same bracket of values. If the resultant figure is out of line with and ahead of the market value, it is highly unlikely that the auctioneers will be successful in generating any interest in that lot.

The report

In the business climate today often the initial inspection and on-site meeting with the client leads straight into the preparation of the auction particulars, so cutting out the traditional report incorporating the recommendations as to the method of sale, fees and costs, and other general matters. However, some clients will still require this form of report for discussion at a board or similar meeting or, if the instructions have come through a solicitor or trustee, in order to refer to other parties.

Remember that this style of report must in essence be concise, to the point, clearly reasoned, and set out under headings for ease of reference.

An overview of the headings which ought to be included in the Report is as follows:

1. Location

2. Description

3. State of repair

4. Services and authorities

5. Local taxes, rates and authorities

6. Planning and development potential

7. Tenure including tenancies/occupiers

8. Market advice

9. The market place

10. Recommendation as to method of sale by auction with supporting reasons

11. Timescale

12. Site, layout, and location plans

13. Caveats.

Referring to caveats, it is dangerous to comment on the condition and state of repair of the property without suitable reservations and also be careful to include additional reservations to preclude the report's being construed as a valuation or being made available to other parties, such as financial institutions.

The auctioneer's terms of engagement

There are two essential threads running through this section. The first is compliance with statute law relating to the disposal of property. The second is to secure the payment of commission and expenses in the event of a dispute.

The 'Guidance Notes for Auctioneers proposing to sell Real Estate at Auction in England and Wales' are published by The Royal Institution of Chartered Surveyors and The Incorporated Society of Valuers & Auctioneers. They are also adopted by The National Association of Estate Agents. These Notes contain essential guidance on various key points which must be covered, preferably in correspondence with the client (see Appendix A).

The important point here is that under current legislation auctions are treated in exactly the same manner as private treaty sales. In the event of a subsequent dispute the agent will have no hope of recovering fees and expenses through the court if the office file is not fully and correctly documented.

The following areas must be covered precisely in correspondence under legislation arising from the Estate Agents Act 1979 and the Statutory Instruments made under this Act. Quoting broadly from the Guidance Notes these are as follows:

1. The type of agency appointment; usually in the case of an auction this is as the Sole Agent or Joint Sole Agent. Remember to include the statutory definition of the type of agency, sole, joint agent or sole selling rights; this is essential.

2. Set out clearly the liability for the vendor to meet the fees and expenses. This must include exactly the circumstances when the liability will arise, and the term/duration of the agency. This section must also include any liability which might arise in the event of a sale prior to the auction or afterwards. It is usual for the auctioneer to include within the timespan of the agency appointment a period of 4 to 6 weeks after the auction sale date.

3. The liability for payment of fees and expenses if the vendor withdraws the instructions between the appointment and the auction date.

4. The rights of the auctioneer to deduct agreed fees and expenses from the deposit. This applies when the deposit is held by the auctioneer.

5. The auctioneer's responsibility and procedure for the reporting of bids prior to the auction.

    Other matters which prudently should be included are:

6. The manner in which the auctioneer may accept deposits; including by cheque or banker's draft.

7. Whether the deposit will be held as stakeholder or agent for the vendor or the purchaser and to whom any interest earned on that deposit accrues; and to whom the balance of the deposit monies shall be sent.

8. The extent of the auctioneer's right

    (a) to refuse bids
    (b) to determine disputes between bidders
    (c) to regulate the bidding increments
    (d) to accept postal, telephone, telex or facsimile bids by way of proxy (with appropriate indemnities from the vendor and the bidder in the event of a failure of communications)
    (e) to release any bidder acting as an agent from personal liability
    (f) to sign the auction contract on behalf of the vendor
    (g) to bid on behalf of the vendor and to advise the vendor not to bid. It is strongly recommended that the auctioneer does not accept instructions where the vendor requires the right to bid up to or over the reserve.

9. The auctioneer's responsibility and procedure for inspections.

10. The auctioneer's right to instruct the vendor's solicitor to undertake all local and other searches and provide special conditions of sale at the vendor's expense and to make all relevant legal documentation available to prospective purchasers.

11. Confirmation from the vendor that any existing instructions to other agents have been withdrawn (excepting those acting as Joint Auctioneers). If Joint Auctioneers are appointed it is advisable for the auctioneer to ensure that the duties and liabilities of the Joint Auctioneer are documented and the basis of remuneration and reimbursement of costs has been agreed.

12. The auctioneer's right to change the venue or date of the auction at his discretion.

13. As the auctioneer does not have implied authority to sell prior or post auction, the circumstances in which the auctioneer is authorised to sign the memorandum of sale on behalf of the vendor.

14. A warranty that the information supplied to the auctioneer by the vendor or the vendor's solicitor or the vendor's managing agents is accurate and an indemnity against liability for inaccuracy.

Additional points which are stated in the Guidance Notes that it is prudent to include are

15. The auctioneer should ask to be notified by the vendor and/or the solicitors of public health notices, local land charges, financial charges, major arrears of rent, disputes and material matters relating to the property being offered for sale.

16. The auctioneer should ask to be notified by the vendor of any sale contemplated by the vendor prior to the auction.

17. The auctioneer should request the vendor to confirm whether or not the sale is subject to VAT and prospective purchasers should be made aware of this fact. It is advisable for the auctioneer to request the vendor to give clear written instructions on the treatment of VAT on the deposit monies.

In the working environment both the Report and the Terms of the Auctioneer's Appointment will usually be sent at the same time to the client. The length of the document forming the Terms of the Auctioneer's appointment will typically today run to some 24 A4 pages, but it is individual to each firm. An extremely wide variation of the style and expression of the basis of the appointment exists, and as yet no standard form has been produced.

4 The Law

This chapter sets out to cover the legal aspects of real property auctions in relation to:

- The Catalogue
- The Auctioneer
- The Bidders
- The Vendor/Seller
- The Purchaser/Buyer
- The General Public

A question often asked of auctioneers is 'Who can be an auctioneer?'. The answer simply is that with few exceptions anyone can set themselves up as an auctioneer, a situation not dissimilar to that for estate agents. The Estate Agents Act 1979 states that the only persons prohibited from carrying out estate agency work are:

1. Persons who have been formally banned under an Order made by the Director General of Fair Trading.
2. A person who has been adjudged bankrupt after 3rd May 1982.

The legislation relating to auctioneering of real property over and above that applicable to estate agency practice is relatively sparse. Rather there is a mixture of statute law, plus enabling regulations and orders, together with case law. However, there are few recent cases which stem from property auctions.

Another source of regulation and control is the creation over many generations of the 'Common Practice' of the landed profession by which property auctions are arranged and conducted. In 1994 The Royal Institution of Chartered Surveyors and The Incorporated Society of Valuers & Auctioneers issued jointly a code of 'best practice' for property auctioneers, referred to as 'Guidance Notes for Auctioneers proposing to sell Real Estate at Public Auction in England and Wales'. This publication was extensively revised and updated in 1998 and it is reproduced in full as Appendix A.

As stated at the outset of this book, it is assumed that the reader is fully conversant with all areas of statutory legislation and case law relating to the sale of property by private treaty. The reader is referred particularly to the Estate Agents Act 1979 and the Regulations and Orders that followed this Act. The Property Misdescriptions Act 1991 and the relevant Orders that followed are also of equal importance.

The following sections of this chapter underscore the specific areas relating to the role of the auction and the auctioneer over and above that relating to the sale by private treaty.

Statute law

1. The Auctioneers Act 1845

2. The Sale of Land by Auction Act 1867

3. The Auctions (Bidding Agreements) Act 1927

4. The Misrepresentation Act 1967

5. Theft Act 1968

6. The Auctions (Bidding Agreements) Act 1969

7. The Unfair Contract Terms Act 1977

8. The Sale of Goods Act 1979

9. The Estate Agents Act 1979 together with the Regulations and the Orders

10. The Landlord and Tenant Act 1987

11. The Property Misdescriptions Act 1991 together with the Orders

12. Money Laundering Regulations 1993

13. Unfair Terms in Consumer Contracts Regulations 1994

14. The Housing Act 1996

The Auctioneers Act 1845

Section 5 of this Act required every auctioneer to have a valid licence, renewable annually, and the fine for failure to comply was the princely sum of £10 and the risk of going to prison for up to one month. This section was repealed by the Finance Act 1949, but a few local authorities have retained the ability to impose trading licences on chattels auctioneers.

Section 7 is still valid and every auctioneer must display in a prominent position a 'ticket or board', in other words a tablet or notice, clearly stating the full first name and surname together with his or her address. Today this takes the form of a standard tablet which the auctioneer hangs in front of the rostrum. The tablet must be on display throughout the whole proceedings of the sale. The fine for failure to display it was originally £20; this was increased to a maximum of £500 under the Criminal Justice Act 1982.

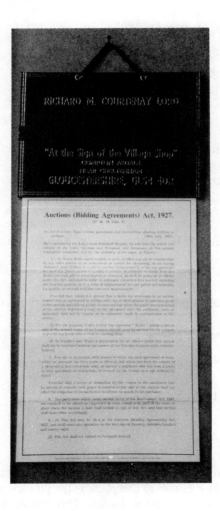

Figure 4.1 The author's auctioneer's tablet as required by Section 7 of the Auctioneers Act 1845

The Sale of Land by Auction Act 1867

Section 5 states that the particulars or conditions of sale will state whether the lot is to be sold subject to reserve or without reserve and whether the right to bid is reserved by the vendor or the auctioneer. Where it is stated that the sale is without reserve, the position is absolutely clear; not only may the vendor not bid, but also the auctioneer, or an agent for the vendor, may not bid. Furthermore, the auctioneer must not knowingly accept bids from the vendor or any representative (agent) bidding on his behalf.

The Act was an attempt to resolve the conflict as between equity and common law, but there was an oversight in the Act.

With regard to the right to bid by the vendor or his agent acting on his behalf the Act remained silent as to whether or not this was limited to the reserve figure or that the right to bid could be exercised above that figure.

Section 6 states that where the conditions of sale or particulars say that the auction is subject to the right of the vendor to bid, the auctioneer, the vendor or any one person may bid.

In simple terms, it appears that where the right is retained to sell a lot subject to a reserve price, then the right to bid must also be expressly stated. However, conversely, where only the right to bid is stipulated, it appears that there is a presumption that there is a reserve price.

The right of the vendor or his agent to bid stems from this legislation and as an extension of this right it is also the authority for the auctioneer to take fictitious bids for the client. However, this right is subject to compliance with strict criteria which are discussed in later chapters.

On examining a set of auction particulars and Conditions of Sale for a lot these rights must be stated clearly to comply with this Act. Typical wording will be: 'Unless otherwise stated the sale is subject to a reserve price', and also 'the vendor and the auctioneers reserve the right to bid on the vendor's own behalf or through an agent at the auction up to, but not in advance of, the reserve price'. A further statement will be: 'the vendor or a person acting on his behalf may bid up to the reserve price.'

It is generally accepted by legal experts that this Act was poorly drafted. The broad result today is:

(a) The auctioneer, vendor or any one person delegated may not bid unless this right has been expressly reserved in the conditions of sale or the particulars.

(b) However, although Section 6 gives the vendor or any one person on his behalf the right to bid where the right is reserved, Section 5 states that where no such right is retained, the vendor may not employ anyone to bid. The issue is whether this can be interpreted to allow personal bidding by the vendor; this awaits an answer at a future date if it is ever tested in the courts.

(c)   Another issue which remains to be decided by the courts is whether the Act
      is a clear statement that a reserve has been fixed.

For further details the reader is referred to Chapter 11 of *Law of Estate
Agency and Auctions* by John Murdoch, 3rd Edition included in the references.

The Auctions (Bidding Agreements) Act 1927

This Act and its counterpart of 1969 were passed primarily to control the auction
ring at chattels sales. As an aside, there have only been two successful
prosecutions under the 1927 Act.
    Section 3 of the Act states that in addition to the notice required in Section 7
of the Auctioneers Act 1845 the auctioneer must also exhibit a copy of this Act.
Failure to comply could result in a fine of £20.
    Today auctioneers comply with this Act by attaching to their tablet, as
required by the Auctioneers Act 1845, a copy of this statute.

The Misrepresentation Act 1967

Where there has been a misrepresentation by the auctioneer or an employee the
purchaser who is able to prove loss can instigate proceedings. The auctioneer
must be careful to check the accuracy of all statements, both written and verbal.
The Act covers civil liability for pre-contractual misstatements which induce
another party to enter into a contract.

The Theft Act 1968

The manner in which the auctioneer conducts the actual auction is discussed in a
later chapter, but there is room for interpretation under this Act to say that an
auctioneer may not take sequential bids on behalf of the vendor client.
    This arises under Section 15 where if deception can be proved by a
purchaser, for example by the auctioneer taking two or more bids 'off the wall',
in other words sequential fictitious bids, then a criminal offence arises. This
situation has not been tested in the courts, but if an action succeeded a criminal
offence would arise, with a penalty of prison up to 10 years or an unlimited fine.
    The issue here is that by taking more than a single bid in succession the
auctioneer has misled other bidders in the room into thinking that more than two
people are genuinely bidding. The thinking is that no one would bid against
themselves, so increasing the price. Interestingly, a contrary view is that in
trading a buyer is always entitled to increase his bid to secure a deal and

therefore consecutive bids are lawful, provided that in the case of property auctions the necessary criteria have been met.

The Auctions (Bidding Agreements) Act 1969

Section 4 states that the auctioneer must exhibit a copy of this Act. Therefore from the beginning of the sale proceedings the auctioneer has to have clearly on show to the company his tablet under the Auctioneers Act 1845, the Auctions (Bidding Agreements) Act 1927, and this Act.

While this Act was placed on the statute books to provide 'teeth' to legislation for the control of auction rings at chattels auctions, it is also applicable to real property auctions. However, to date there has been no prosecution involving a real property auction, although there has been concern expressed that there is the remote possibility of a ring operating at collective sales.

The Unfair Contract Terms Act 1977

The vendor client, the agent, and the purchaser are all encompassed in this Act. The legislation introduces the test of 'reasonableness' in relation to any clauses which seek to limit or exclude liability. The interpretation of reasonableness is not to be confused with fairness, but under an EC Directive we now have overlapping legislation since the latter introduces a new test of fairness! The Department of Trade and Industry Regulations implementing the EC Directive on Unfair Terms in Consumer Contracts came into force on 1 July 1995.

The Act does not apply to contracts relating to the sale or lease of real property, but it does apply to agency contracts, and therefore the relation between the estate agent and the client.

The Regulations which came into force on 1 July 1995 apply to terms which have not been individually negotiated and apply to many forms of contract. Real property transactions are not excluded and so the General and Special Conditions of Sale at auction are included within the scope of the regulations.

Here the burden lies with the auctioneer to demonstrate that the terms have been individually negotiated and that the terms of the contract are in plain intelligible language. The test is fairness as opposed to reasonableness set out in the 1977 Act.

The Sale of Goods Act 1979

Certain elements of this Act require auctioneers to be on their guard when offering furnished parts of offices and homes. This applies where the purchase price or separate consideration under the terms of the contract involve the transfer of ownership of goods and equipment.

The Estate Agents Act 1979

While this Act and the subsequent regulations and orders are familiar to all those involved in agency, there are certain sections which have a direct bearing on the auctioneer. The legislation stemming from this Act through the attendant Regulations and Orders regulates the work of the estate agent in all areas of agency activity, residential, commercial, industrial, land and agriculture. It provides a number of limited controls, but as John Murdoch states in Chapter 6 of *Law of Estate Agency and Auctions* '...these controls fall a long way short of anything resembling an overall code'.

Section 13 refers to the holding of client's money. The Act creates a statutory trust and protects monies held by an agent against claims by general creditors. The trust is strictly for the benefit of persons entitled to demand the money from the estate agent.

Section 14 relates to the maintenance of accounts. The Act is specific and states that, where money is held on behalf of a client, it must be promptly paid into a 'client account'. The Account Regulations set out clearly how the actual accounts and records are to be maintained.

Section 15 deals with interest on monies held by the auctioneer. The auctioneer, where the deposit is held as agent for one party as opposed to stakeholder, is liable to pay and account for the interest earned on the deposit. This obligation arises where the deposit exceeds £500 and the interest on that sum is at least £10.

However, this Section provides for an 'arrangement in writing, when-ever made' for the obligation to be modified or excluded as to interest.

Section 21 requires the disclosure of all personal interests not only of the auctioneer, but also his staff and those of their families and a wide circle of relations. This relates not only to present but also possible future interests. The auctioneer must be aware that the definition of 'personal interest' in the Act is wide.

In summary the following broad areas are covered:

- Information to the vendor client – details of charges, special commission clauses, the nature of the agency.

- Other duties to the client – variation of the terms of the agency, information regarding services requested by purchasers, notification of offers received, disclosure of personal interests.

- Duties to third parties – misrepresentation of offers, discrimination over services, disclosure of personal interests.

- Client's money – restrictions on taking deposits, accounts and records, interest on deposits.

- Restrictions on the right to practice – prohibition orders, bankruptcy, and minimum standards of competence.

The Landlord and Tenant Act 1987 and The Housing Act 1996

The Landlord and Tenant Act 1987 relates to sales of residential invest-ments and ground rents. It does not apply to mixed users where more than 50% of the internal floor area is non-residential. The Act gave tenants of some types of residential property the right of first refusal to buy when the landlord decided to sell. As there were no penalties for failure to comply with the Act, it was largely ignored and auctioneers merely stated that notices had not been served on the tenants. A typical clause reads: 'The seller has not served notices under Section 5 of the Landlord and Tenant Act 1987 and the purchaser takes with full knowledge thereof.'

Any property with two or more flats where more than half the flats are rented or leased fall within the Act. The right of first refusal comes into operation on any disposal by a landlord of any estate or interest other than those excepted by the Act. Section 1 provides that landlords shall not 'make a relevant disposal' unless they have first served a statutory notice incorporating provisions set out in Section 5.

Such a notice must:

- Contain particulars of the principal terms of the disposal.

- State that the offer constitutes an offer to dispose of the property to a majority of the qualifying tenants.

- Specify a period of not less than two months within which the tenants and lessees can accept the offer.

- Specify a further period of not less than two months in which the majority of qualifying tenants may nominate a person or persons to accept the offer.

The notice must be served on 90% of all tenants or lessees.

This Act has now been the subject of substantial changes as a result of the Housing Act 1996.

Section 89 of the Housing Act 1996 provides that a landlord has committed a criminal offence if, without reasonable excuse, he makes a relevant disposal without first having served notice under section 5 of the Landlord and Tenant Act 1987. There is no definition of 'reasonable excuse', so this awaits interpretation by the courts.

Since 1 October 1996 the law has been amended by the Housing Act 1996 to allow landlords wishing to sell qualifying investment property an alternative route of disposal, namely a sale by public auction.

Where the landlord proposes to make a relevant disposal by auction, notice must be served not less than four months, nor more than six months, before the date of the auction. This notice must contain particulars of the principal terms of the disposal and state that the disposal is to be by way of auction. The notice constitutes an offer by the landlord to the tenants for the auction contract to have effect as if a purchaser nominated by the tenants had signed the auction contract rather than the successful bidder.

The tenants have a period of not less than two months to accept this offer (and this period must end not less than two months before the auction), and a further 28 days to nominate a purchaser (and this period must not be less than 28 days before the auction).

If the time and place of the auction is not provided, the tenants must be notified not less than 28 days before the date of the sale.

If the tenants do not nominate a person to represent them, or they inform the landlord that they do not wish to proceed with the acquisition, the landlord may then dispose of his interest at auction, but only within 12 months of the end of the period in which the tenants may appoint a representative or the landlord is notified that the tenants do not wish to proceed. After the 12 month period the clock will start running again.

A person nominated by the tenants must elect, not less than 28 days before the auction, that the provisions of Schedule 6 will apply. If this is done and the property submitted to auction, the landlord must, within seven days of the sale at auction, send a copy of the contract to the nominated person who then has 28 days to decide whether or not to accept the auction contract. If he accepts the contract, in effect he becomes the buyer. The completion of the sale cannot take place less than 28 days after the day upon which the nominated purchaser is deemed to have entered into the auction contract.

The Act does not provide that the successful bidder at the auction has no claim for breach of contract and damages against the landlord as a result of his failure to complete the contracted sale. There is a need to absolve the seller for any consequences of the Act in the special conditions of sale to provide for this situation.

The purchaser will know whether or not the tenants have indicated their acceptance of the landlord's offer. Their decision to proceed will depend upon the price paid under the auctioneer's gavel. The practical effect of this will be little different to the old regime. Under the 1987 Act, if the landlord sells at auction in breach of his statutory duty, the tenants are entitled to serve a purchase notice requiring the new landlord to convey the same interest to them on the same terms. In fact, under the 1996 Act the purchaser will be better off. He will not have to complete the sale and so avoids stamp duty and further legal fees.

Simply selling subject to a condition to the effect that this Act has not been complied with and that the purchaser takes the lot with full knowledge thereof, as has been the practice, will no longer be sufficient to avoid the weight of the new Act.

Many auctioneers who are active in this field are now serving the required notices on the tenants themselves at the outset of their appointment as auctioneer. This means effectively a delay of some 4 months while the various steps as stipulated by the Housing Act 1996 are followed through.

There were excellent articles on this subject in the *Estates Gazette* on 30 August 1996 (issue 9635) by Gary Murphy and on 7 September 1996 (issue 9636) by Jane Fox-Edwards.

The Property Misdescriptions Act 1991

While this Act does not change the civil law it creates a criminal offence. Generally all auctioneer's particulars form part of the Conditions of Sale and Contract.

Consequently, any misdescription in the particulars may entitle the aggrieved purchaser to recision of the contract or at least damages. This will also include any statements included in the Auctioneer's Addendum to the Particulars or made by the auctioneer from the rostrum at the commencement of the auction.

The Act rules that an offence is committed when a false or misleading statement about a 'prescribed' matter is made. These 'prescribed' matters are listed and there are 33 of them as set out in the 1992 Order. An offence arises irrespective of whether or not it was made innocently, negligently or fraudulently. However, there is a defence to show that a person took all reasonable steps to avoid committing the offence. The Act states that 'false' is to be interpreted as false to a material degree.

For the auctioneer, areas to be especially on guard against, over and above private treaty sales, include 'puffing statements' from the rostrum, photographs, plans, artists' impressions, price guides, and interpretation of lease terms.

Useful guidance on the application of this Act will be found in the Manual of Estate Agency Law and Practice which is currently in the draft stage. Publication by RICS Books is expected in the summer of 1998.

Money Laundering Regulations 1993

These relate to the potential use of property auctions to transfer illegal funds into real property. Auctioneers have a duty to report any suspected transactions to the appropriate authorities.

Unfair Terms in Consumer Contracts Regulations 1994

Refer to the section on the Unfair Contract Terms Act 1997, page 35.

Case law

Below is set out a selection of relevant cases. However, remember that this is an area of constantly changing emphasis and interpretation as fresh case law is established through decisions being handed down by the courts. Current reading and updating is essential.

Museprime Properties Ltd and Adhill Properties Ltd 1990
Here an indication was given that rent reviews remained outstanding. They had in fact been fixed and the purchaser was allowed to rescind.

Atlantic Estates Ltd and Ezekiel 1991
The photograph of the lot in the catalogue showed a sign saying 'wine bar by day, cocktail bar by night' and this was instrumental to the purchaser buying. In fact the tenant had lost his liquor licence and the purchaser was allowed to rescind.
    The court confirmed that there was no defence for the vendor to say that the purchaser could have discovered this fact by making enquiries.

King Brothers (Finance) and North Western British Road Services Ltd 1986
The contract was rescinded when a property, described as industrial premises of 50,000 square feet *with* vehicle inspection pits, paint spray booths and ancillary accommodation, in fact turned out to be 36000 square feet of workshops *including* the pits and booths and 11000 square feet of ancillary buildings.

Rignall Developments and Halil 1987
The court considered failure to disclose the existence of a housing improvement grant. This was held to be a defect in the title and grounds for recision.

Production Technology Consultants and Bartlett 1988
The fact that documents are available for inspection before the auction provides little protection. Here the auction particulars stated that the property was subject

to a regulated tenancy when in fact it was subject to a 99 year lease. The documents showing the true position were available but the purchaser had not inspected them. The court set aside the contract.

McCullagh and Lane Fox & Partners Ltd 1994

It was held that the vendor's agent owes a duty of care to the purchaser. Here, the size of the garden of the house was overstated. Despite this, it was held that the purchaser had not relied on this misstatement having walked the boundaries of the site and happily proceeded with the contract. The purchaser failed to have the contract rescinded for this reason.

Cremdean Properties Ltd v·Nash 1977

Joint vendors were selling by tender a block of city centre property for redevelopment as offices with outline planning permission. It transpired that because of an alleged misrepresentation the actual office space was substantially less than stated in the particulars. The agents had stated in the special conditions that the accuracy of the particulars were not guaranteed and that any intending purchaser must satisfy themselves by inspection or otherwise. The agents had the full authority of their clients to draw up the documents and the court was trying the preliminary issue of whether or not the existence of the condition conclusively negated any misrepresentation. The Court of Appeal rejected this view. Section 3 of the Misrepresentation Act 1967 applied to the purported disclaimer and only at a full trial could it be decided whether or not it was fair and reasonable.

A further issue was examined, namely whether a disclaimer is part of the contract or merely a preliminary misrepresentation. The view was that in this case if the disclaimer was a term of the contract binding on the parties, then it was counter to section 3 of the Act and ineffective unless the court thought that it was fair and reasonable to give it effect. On the other hand if it was not part of the contract, then it was not binding on the purchaser.

The case highlights the tendency today to consider with suspicion any steps which are taken by agents to shelter behind disclaimer clauses. Section 3 of the Misrepresentation Act 1967 is a formidable hurdle for a vendor to jump. The case is reported at length in Chapter 9, pages 272 to 274, of *Auctions Law and Practice* by Brian Harvey and Franklin Meisel.

South Western Property Co. Ltd v Marton 1982

A parcel of land was sold by auction, being described in the particulars as long leasehold building land. It was held that although a range of disclaimer clauses were included in the particulars and conditions of sale, these did not pass the test of reasonableness and judgment was granted in favour of the plaintiff.

Overbrooke Estates Ltd v Glencombe Properties Ltd 1974
It was established that vendors are entitled to draw the attention of the public to
the limits placed on the authority of their agents. The auctioneer has no authority
to give representations or warranties on behalf of the vendor.

St Marylebone Property Co. Ltd v Payne 1994
Another case involving photographs where the arrow on the photograph gave the
impression that the property was larger than it was. The contract was rescinded
and the deposit refunded.

A case relating to auctions is Mainguild Ltd trading as Winkworth
Auctioneers and London Borough of Croydon Trading Standards Office. This
was among the first 50 prosecutions under the Property Misdescriptions Act
1991 where there was a misstatement relating to a flat which was on the third
floor, but advertised and sold as being on the second floor. The auctioneers were
fined £250 with £336 costs.

As will be seen from the content of this chapter the law relating to property
auctions is spread widely through various statutes, case law and common
practice. For further reading the following are recommended:

Auctions Law and Practice by Brian W. Harvey and Franklin Meisel. Second
Edition, 1995, Oxford University Press.

Law of Estate Agency and Auctions by John Murdoch. Third Edition, 1994, The
Estates Gazette Ltd.

Estates Gazette. Published weekly and containing both a special auction section
and from time to time articles on procedures, law and other matters relating to
auctions (see References and Further Reading).

Something which may puzzle the reader, and not a few auctioneers, is the
legal authority on which the control of the bidding together with the increments
of bids and the right to refuse bids originates. The answer appears to rest with
common law and for each sale the auctioneer and the vendor client solicitor will
embody standard clauses in the Conditions of Sale. These conditions seek to
govern the basis of the legal relationship between not only the auctioneer and the
vendor client, but also the purchaser and the other bidders. The usual reference
source which sets out the authority of the auctioneer on these and other matters
is 'The Standard Conditions of Sale' (Third Edition), first published in March
1990 by The Solicitors' Law Stationery Society Limited. However it is
understood that some auction houses use their own Conditions of Sale and each
set of sale particulars merits detailed examination as they follow similar lines but
with important variations. The 1997 Annual Report of ISVA, issued in February
1998, states that the Auctioneering Committee has taken forward the preparation
of a standard set of General Conditions of Sale which could be adopted by all

real property auctioneers in the country. This statement underlines the existence and current use of a range of Conditions of Sale and the desirability for standardisation.

5 The File and Particulars

The auction file

The auction file is the central clearing house of an auction. There must be a file for each lot for ease of quick reference by all members of the staff and these files need to be kept up to date on a daily basis. Here will be recorded all the detailed information. Today these files are computer based and each firm will have their own tailor-made software package for handling their particular type and style of auction. Every firm maintains files of correspondence for each lot together with computer records. A typical document on the computer will contain:

- Auctioneer's Reference
- Lot Number
- Address
- Client
- Joint Agent
- Solicitor
- Commission Fee
- Entry Fee

A check sheet which at a glance shows the current position of the vital stages in preparing and proceeding through the various steps leading from the initial instruction through to the actual sale is a practical *aide-mémoire*. This saves endless wasted minutes rifling the files to establish exactly the current position as to printing, advertising and all other relevant details. A blank example for a single lot country auction is included at the end of the chapter. For multi-lot and collective sales the layout will follow a very different pattern, but the principle remains the same. Easy access to the vital information as to the state of play when preparing the auction is essential.

Every aspect of the auction particulars has to be checked and double checked since once the particulars are printed the cost and time wasted in issuing an Addendum of the Particulars to everyone who received the original copies can be considerable; it must also be done to comply with the law. Particular care must be taken with respect to the provisions of the Property Misdescriptions Act 1991. The laborious task of checking the details and accuracy of the information finally rest at the door of the auctioneer of that lot, but with major collective sales the role will devolve down the team and even extend to Joint Auctioneers and with repossessed properties to local agents.

The auction date and attendance by solicitors

Major auctioneers who regularly hold sales will have a list of sale dates running at least one year ahead, and these slots will have been agreed with the other auctioneers in their city or town. It is in no-one's interest to have a clash of dates. For local regional sales it is sensible to check with other firms before settling on a particular date.

If it is desired to have the vendor's solicitors in attendance at the auction, check that the date is convenient to them.

The auction particulars

Following the preparation of the initial draft of the particulars the auctioneer needs to go through them line by line confirming that all the content is both accurate and factual. The following areas are the most frequent pitfalls which can give rise to problems:

1. Measurement: Check that the lot has been referenced in accordance with the joint *RICS & ISVA Code of Measuring Practice*, Fourth Edition.

The introduction to the Code states 'Long established and understood professional obligations to clients are now matched by additional statutory obligations to users of property. With effect from 4th April 1993, it is a criminal offence for those involved in estate agency or property development business to give false or misleading information about specified aspects of land (which includes buildings) which are offered for sale. In this context, the Property Misdescriptions Act 1991 and the Property Misdescriptions (Specified Matters) Order 1992 specifically refer to measurements and sizes.'

The Code goes on to say: 'Measurements (and floor areas or sizes), if they are stated, must be accurate. They must not mislead. Accurate measurement is a matter of fact; it is not a matter of opinion. Surveyors should aim to achieve accuracy, and not work to what they believe to be acceptable tolerances.'

Remember that from 1 January 1995 it is mandatory to provide measurements, sizes etc. in metric units, although until 31 December 1999 it is permissible also to quote imperial units.

2. Tenure: Obtain written confirmation of the tenure and copies of leases, agreements and licences.

With leases, agreements and licences these must be checked in detail against the information which was obtained from all other quarters.

Where the information was originally obtained from managing agents or the landlard it is essential to check that the details agree in every respect with the documentation, and if there are any variations these must be resolved at once. All this information must be checked with the vendor's solicitors.

3. Rental Incomes and Rent Reviews: Always read through the lease, agreements, and licences to confirm that the details as set out in your schedules are correct.

Again double check that the rents passing agree with your schedules and that rent review dates are also correct, and as a final check again obtain confirmation from the vendor's solicitors.

Remember to comply with the Housing Act 1996 and attendant legislation over notices to tenants of residential investment properties.

4. Boundaries: Make certain that the boundaries which are shown on your plan coincide with those on the title deeds or lease. Also, where possible confirm the liability for maintenance of the boundaries and their ownership. Where these are not known, then state this fact.

Typical of the problems which occur here are where there has been encroachment, often due to lack of stout fencing on the ground, ditches and watercourses have been infilled and where major development has taken place alongside with new walls and fences incorrectly aligned.

5. Rights of Way and Easements: From your site inspection some of these may be obvious, but all too frequently these are not apparent on site. Check with both the solicitors and the Local Authority so that on file is a record of both public and other rights of way and easements. The types of easements are numerous and may include water, telephone, gas, electricity, drainage (foul and storm), water courses, and specialist services. Remember that the easements may not only be on the surface but also underground and so not visible from a site inspection.

6. Private Roads: Often service roads and lanes are in other ownership which is not always apparent from site inspection. Here it is important to establish the ownership and any liability for maintenance and upkeep as there may not necessarily be an annual charge.

7. Services: After the site inspection confirm with the various suppliers in writing the details of the various services. With country property where there may be a private water supply, check on its reliability, and on any easements or agreements and charges. Usually it is prudent to confirm with the local authority that the supply is fit for human consumption, and in some cases that the appropriate licence for abstraction is in force.

In many rural and isolated country areas drainage may be by a private system, such as a septic tank, cesspool, or an individual sewerage plant. Establish whether or not the installation is within the ownership of the property, and if not whether or not the appropriate easements are in place.

If the system is shared with other property check on the arrangements for sharing the costs of upkeep, as often for older installations the deeds are silent.

With commercial and investment properties these checks are not usually undertaken by the auctioneers. Rather the agent relies on the purchasers to make their own enquiries and the particulars are silent on services.

8. Plans: Be careful how the extracts of Ordnance Survey plans are trimmed. They must fairly represent the locality and so by choosing to trim the plan to omit a railway line, major road, factory, school, or retail centre can be said to be misleading.

Delete all irrelevant information on the plan so that it is clear and clean in presentation. Confirm that there is a north point and scale. On the latter point bear in mind that plans usually alter as to scale in printing so make sure that a 'caveat' is included. A typical 'caveat' will read 'For identification purposes only'.

A wider 'caveat' embracing both plans and photographs reads:

'All location plans shown in the Particulars in this catalogue are to enable prospective purchasers to locate the property only. The plans are photo-graphically reproduced and therefore not to scale and are not intended to depict the interest to be disposed of. Such plans are expressly excluded from the contract of sale or other disposal referred to in this catalogue.

Any arrows on photographs or plans in the Particulars in this catalogue are to enable prospective purchasers to locate the property and are not intended to depict the interest or extent thereof to be disposed of.

No warranty or undertaking is given as to the accuracy of the photographs indicating the property proposed to be sold.

No warranty or undertaking is given that the photograph of the relevant property shows or refers to any of the occupiers of the property or whether any of the occupiers are trading or whether any tenant is in actual occupation, the state or condition of such property, at the date of sale or at any time after the date of the publication of this catalogue.

Prospective purchasers must rely on inspection of the property concerned and the Special Conditions in the catalogue as to the full description and extent of the area of the relevant property to be sold.

No warranty or undertaking is given that any of the trading entities shown in any street trader plan is trading or is in actual occupation of the relevant property. Prospective purchasers must satisfy themselves in this respect.

Location plans reproduced in this catalogue are based on Ordnance Survey Maps with the sanction of the Controller of H.M. Stationery Office. Crown Copyright reserved.'

All reproductions of Ordnance Survey plans and maps can only be reproduced under a licence obtainable from H.M. Stationery Office and the reproduction must contain an acknowledgement to this effect. The printing of the acknowledgement is not sufficient in itself and without the necessary licence the Crown copyright is infringed.

9. Artists' impressions: Where these are used make certain that the drawing is consistent with the detailed planning consent. Furthermore, when detailed consent has not been granted, then it is sensible not to use any artistic impressions.

Where they are used, the approval of the architect that the drawing is consistent with the detailed planning consent is essential together with his or her consent to its use in the catalogue.

10. Photographs: Take care to ensure that they show the property fairly, and as with plans ensure that they are not angled or trimmed to exclude something in close proximity which might influence a prospective buyer; for example overhead power lines, a motorway or an adjoining factory in relation to a residential property.

When arrows are used to show the extent of the lot, take great care to be accurate, and beware of the situation where the ownership does not follow a simple vertical division.

In the use of aerial photographs again take care where boundaries are imposed.

11. Planning Consents: Always obtain copies of the relevant consents and check that, where the approved works have not been carried out, the consent will still be valid at the date of the auction. Where conditions are attached to the consent and the work has been carried out, check that it complies.

Where there is a planing history it is important to ensure that the file has copies of all the consents and refusals, together with the relevant correspondence and other documents, including plans and drawings.

In all instances the original documents should be held by the vendor's solicitors.

12. Statutory Notices and Orders: Again obtain copies and look at the dates and time spans for action, especially when set against the auction date. This applies especially to outline and detailed planning consents.

13. Rural frontage strips: With country lots always carefully confirm by reference to the conveyance plan that the ownership extends up to the public highway. In some locations the verge or frontage strip may not be shown on the deeds as within the ownership and here there may be a ransom strip owned by an estate.

14. Roads: Never assume that the road accesses are public highways. Obtain confirmation that the roads are made up and adopted by the Highway Authority.

With urban properties, ownership of the lot may extend to the centre of the public highway.

15. Viewing: Confirm the arrangements and bear in mind that there will be hopefully the need for a large number of interested bidders to have access over a relatively short period of time. In addition, there will be the requirement for surveyors, engineers, and specialist contractors to have access, often for periods of a half day or more.

16. Furnishings and Equipment: Where part of the property is furnished or there is equipment included, make certain that it complies with any relevant statutory legislation; for example soft furnishings and electrical appliances in residential property.

17. Price Guides: This is usually a genuine indication of the likely realisation price. Furthermore if it is below the eventual price at which the reserve is fixed, it is likely to amount to a misleading statement under the provisions of the Property Misdescriptions Act 1991. Do not confuse the reserve price with the sale price here; it is the relationship of the Price Guide to the reserve which is important.

The meaning or definition of Price Guide should be defined in the particulars, catalogue or Price Guide list. It may not necessarily be a genuine indication of the likely sale price as that will depend upon various factors which come into play on the sale day. A typical auction catalogue may state that the Price Guides are an indication of the minimum acceptable sale price to each vendor, that they should not be interpreted as asking prices and that they are purely for guidance. Each one is stated as 'subject to contract'.

For further reading please refer to Chapter 9.

18. Prior Sales: For a sale to be contracted before an auction, the right to sell
     under these circumstances must be stated clearly in the particulars and in all
     advertising.

Generally, once these steps and checks have been completed the draft
particulars are sent to both the vendor client and their solicitors for approval. Be
on your guard not to accept amendments as to the manner in which your client
may wish the lot to be described as the auctioneer must have absolute faith in the
descriptions and representations.

When writing to the solicitors it is usual to ask them to undertake the
searches and obtain the Enquiries on Contract from the vendor. This information
needs to be available once the particulars are circulated.

Once the draft particulars are returned duly approved by the vendor client
and the solicitors, any amendments which are acceptable to the auctioneers are
incorporated and the printing is put in hand.

An important point is that the auction particulars are read as part of the
Conditions of Sale, and as such form part of the contract. Absolute accuracy is
therefore essential.

Always check throughout the particulars for consistency on spellings, names,
and colours together with typefaces and emphasis.

With Collective Sales consider whether or not a location plan should be
included together with directions from the main roads and station to the sale
venue.

Another point is to check that Joint Agents are fairly and consistently
represented in the catalogue.

When the printed particulars are returned from the printers they are
circulated to all the applicants on the office mailing list. At the same time copies
are sent out to the vendor client, the solicitors and for regional sales the venue.
Another target for circulation, which may come as a surprise to some, is fellow
estate agents. After all the auctioneer is a sole agent and the wider that the net is
cast the better!

The checklist and route for the preparation for a single lot is the same as that
for a multi-lot sale where inevitably the attention to detail is all the greater.

Disclaimer clauses

A disclaimer clause may be an effective defence against an action under the
Misrepresentation Act 1967, but this will not help if an offence is proved under
the Property Misdescriptions Act 1991. The value and use of disclaimer clauses
in any event will depend to some degree upon the style and manner by which
they are expressed in the auction particulars. They are best printed in the same
size and type-style as the content to which they relate. The broad view is that
disclaimer clauses should be incorporated in the particulars or catalogue as they

still carry weight. However, the clauses must be reasonable in all circumstances having regard to the Unfair Contract Terms Act 1977 and liability for a criminal offence cannot be excluded.

Types of auction particulars

These range widely depending upon the type of sale. At the one end of the spectrum is the extended version of private treaty particulars which include the information and general remarks on the auction, together with a plan. For a small collective sale with a few lots the auctioneer will usually prepare individual auction particulars for each lot.

For the larger collective sales the auction particulars will be presented as a catalogue incorporating all the lots. These auction catalogues are impressive documents often containing several hundred lots and make fascinating reading. They will include in addition to the descriptions, photographs where appropriate, location and site plans, General and Special Conditions of Sale, auction price guides, the Memorandum and Proxy Bid forms.

Whether or not the General and Special Conditions of Sale and Memorandum of Sale are printed with the individual lot particulars or in the catalogue is a matter to be decided by the auctioneer. There are strong reasons for the case that these are printed as part of the auction particulars. If this is done then all the documentation is available to all the interested parties from the outset.

However, the practical problem with single lot sales is that the production of these documents usually takes too long and will delay the printing of the particulars for circulation. This is why commonly the 'General Remarks' in the auction particulars will state that the legal documents will be available at the auctioneer's office and those of the vendor's solicitors fourteen days prior to the sale date. This situation is not entirely satisfactory because the end result is that the auctioneer has to deal with enquiries on a piecemeal basis and all too easily a vital detail can be overlooked. In these circumstances all enquiries are best directed through the office of the solicitors and a file note made to this effect.

Auction Action Sheet

Property: ....

....**Post Code**...........

Client ....

         Contact......................................**Tel/Fax**...............**Ext**..............

Client Address..

....**Post Code**.......

Solicitors ....

....**Post Code**.......

         Contact......................................**Tel/Fax**...............**Ext**..............

Sale Date...................**Time**........................**Confirmed**............

Sale Venue ....

         Date booked...........................

         Contact......................................**Tel/Fax**

         Confirmed..............

DRAFT PARTICULARS & PLAN

  Solicitors   **Client**

  To..........**From**..............   **To**............**From**...............

PRINTERS.............................   **Contact**..............

         Tel/Fax.......................**Ext**.....................

Partic & Plan   **Photos**   **Poster**

To...................   ....

Proof..............   ....

Returned.......   ....

CIRCULATION

	Client	Solicitor	Venue	Offices	M/L
Particulars	....	....	....	....	....
Posters	....	....	....	....	

STATUTORY BODIES

Planning	Footpaths	Drain	Water	Gas	Elec	Telephone
....Sent
....Rec'd

ADDENDA   **Circulated to:**

Checked by	Solicitor	Client	M/L	Known Bidders
....	....	....	....	....

Auctioneer...............**Sale Board**   Yes/No   **Acc.No**..................

---

6 Types of Auction

Auction sales fall broadly into three categories. The individual lot, small collective sales of up to a dozen lots, and major collective sales often running into several hundred properties. The last group will be offered in London and major regional centres.

The individual auction – Single lot sales

This type of auction sale is where only one property is offered for sale. In some rural areas the traditional manner for handling the sale of a cottage and its contents may still be found. Here the auctioneer attends at the property on the sale day and first offers by auction the property and then follows on immediately with the contents. The benefits for both the vendor client and the auctioneer are that there will be a large crowd of local residents creating a friendly relaxed atmosphere into which the would-be bidders for the property can submerge themselves.

The scene on the morning of the auction with the auctioneer standing on his or her box by the front door with the contents laid out on the surrounding lawns and vegetable garden, the nearby field and lanes jammed with parked cars and vans is all part of the makings of a successful sale day.

It is here, as always, that the auctioneer needs to have alongside him or her when offering the property the manager or negotiator who has dealt with all the enquiries and viewings, as that person will be able to point out to the auctioneer before the auction proceedings begin which potential bidders and their agents are present. It goes without saying that the local auctioneer will also know the solicitors active in property matters who may well have come along to bid on behalf a client.

However, sadly the scene painted in the preceding paragraphs is one from the past and largely died out in the late 1970s. Today the usual route for auctioning a single lot is to hold the sale in the local village inn, suburban public house or the local hall in the evening at 6 pm or 6.30 pm. The latter time of 6.30 pm is preferable as this allows sufficient time for everyone to come along after work and to charge their glasses, so generating a convivial and relaxed ambience to the sale. From the auctioneer's and solicitor's viewpoint it gives time for questions to be asked and for any problems or loose ends to be tied up before the sale starts, so avoiding being faced with awkward questions at the beginning of the auction.

Another route for the single lot is to offer it at the nearest main hotel, agricultural club or similar venue associated with auction sales in the locality. The problem here is that many of the local residents will not be tempted to come along and the company invariably will be made up of only genuinely interested parties. What auctioneers refer to as 'the free valuation brigade' will be absent! This type of auction tends to be purely a business transaction and for the auctioneer it may be difficult to generate the atmosphere of the auction.

Collective auctions

Here the auctioneer will have generated a number of lots to be sold, possibly all originating from one vendor, but usually from several different sources. The fact that the lots are all different in value and type does not matter. In fact to some degree it is preferable, as the sale will attract a wide range of bidders and if care is taken over the lotting, disappointed bidders on one lot will have the opportunity to try for another lot. In any event from the auctioneer's standpoint the larger the attendance the better as this gives plenty of opportunity to conduct a lively sale.

A glance through the pages of a current copy of *Estates Gazette* in the auction section will give an instant snapshot of the wide range of vendors and types of lots coming forward for sale. Examples include:

Halifax plc	Woolwich plc
Britannia Building Society	Mountview Estates plc
The Inland Revenue	Ladbrooke Racing Limited
British Telecommunications plc	Court of Protection
Lloyds Bank plc	Heritage Hotels Limited
The Secretary of State for Transport	British Waterways Board
The London Borough of Waltham Forest	Norwich City Council

The list appears to be endless and the lots range in value from a few thousand pounds in value upward to million pound plus. Usually the sales will include a strong element of private vendors and mortgagees in possession, receivers, trustees, public and private companies.

The venue needs to be somewhere that is easy to find, with adequate parking, good access and a natural route directly to the sale room. Any venue with a tortuous route from the car park to the sale room, perhaps involving stairs, is not satisfactory. The room needs to be large enough to accommodate those attending, space for completion of the legal formalities, and ideally a side room with refreshments laid on.

As mentioned the collective sale has the great advantage of offering a wide range of property on one day, often and preferably including several similar lots in each category. This gives choice and the chance to bid for alternative properties, so encouraging the maximum number of people to come along to the auction. Anyone who has attended a major collective sale will have sensed the businesslike atmosphere of the room, the feeling that those present are intent about their business and the competitiveness, all excellent ingredients towards a successful auction.

Depending upon the number and type of lots the venue will be selected according to the criteria mentioned above and it is sensible to follow the local tradition where this has already been established. In major provincial centres and in London auctioneers have frequently created particular venues associated with their auction house and for a new entry into this field the auctioneer may decide to establish a fresh venue which will become associated with their name.

The sale time and day will be determined by local tradition, the number of lots, and whether the sale is to span more than one day, or be divided into specialist categories. Likewise, whether or not a morning or afternoon sale is to be conducted is a matter for the auctioneer to decide.

Lotting of property for sale

The approach here is the same as the advice which would be given on the sale of any property. The auctioneer has to take into account all factors which will ensure that the best advice is given with the aim of achieving the optimum overall realisation figure.

Such factors relate to interest from adjoining owners and occupiers, planning potential and consents, and different uses of each part of the property.

The classic case is the property with land, not necessarily all within the curtilage. Here the main property may be lotted separately, with adjoining land, say a paddock, as a second lot, and the plot across the road with consent for a dwelling as a third lot.

Similar and more challenging is a parade of shops in a secondary position with a double unit at one end which has an owner occupier. The balance to be struck is whether or not a premium bid from that occupier if the shop is lotted separately will achieve an overall higher realisation figure.

Lotting will rely on the knowledge of the auctioneer and is determined at the stage when the auction particulars are being prepared. From a practical point of view it is perhaps better to lot separately if in doubt, as subsequently at the time of the sale lots can always be amalgamated. In the final analysis the lotting will be discussed and agreed with the vendor client.

Remember that lotting does not necessarily determine the order of sale, but rather keeps the options open for a decision immediately before the sale. The object, as stated at the beginning of this section, is to stimulate the maximum amount of interest with the aim of achieving the optimum realisation figure under the hammer. Always be on your guard, as one thing you can be certain of, is that a developer or speculator will always be on the lookout for the badly lotted property and the opportunity to buy at auction and then promptly divide it up and sell on at a profit.

Order of sale

As with any auction the secret for a successful sale is to keep the main body of
bidders present throughout the proceedings. Likewise, it is a good idea to get the
sale off to a flying start with the first lot providing plenty of competitive bidding
leading to a resounding hammer price. This sets the tone for the remainder of
the sale.

When planning the order in which the lots will be offered decisions as to
whether or not to mix different types of property depend upon the number of lots
making up the sale. It is generally sensible to bring together in groups specific
types and users and, within those groups, like values. This will encourage
bidders to attend for the appropriate part of the sale and hopefully for the
auctioneer the underbidders will go on to bid for other lots.

Another element is the known bidder. For example, if they are likely to buy
Lot 1, then that bidder may well be anxious to secure the adjoining paddock, so
logically this becomes Lot 2. Now, assuming that just down the lane is another
paddock, this logically becomes Lot 3. The theory is to retain the competitive
interest of the presumed purchaser of Lot 1 through any subsequent lots which
he may wish to buy in competition against other bidders. This generates the
possibility of achieving that 'premium' price.

The Order of Sale, although set out in the Auction Particulars, can be varied
on the sale day. However, the auctioneer must make this possibility crystal clear
at the outset by stating this fact, usually as a separate clause in the Particulars.
Often it is not feasible to be absolutely categoric at the time of going into print
on the order of sale, because individual interest and its strength is unknown and
will only become apparent during the marketing.

With major collective sales the Order of Sale is determined at the time of
preparation of the sale catalogue and, except where lots have been sold prior or
withdrawn, the auction will follow the catalogue.

London and regional centres

Not surprisingly, there are two opposing points of view on the merits or
otherwise of selling locally, regionally and in London. The regional auctioneer
will stoutly defend the local sale and equally the London auction houses will
point strongly to the benefits of selling certain types of lots at major collective
auctions.

All will agree that there are sound reasons for both routes and that there are
some lots which are best sold either locally or nationally. However, there is a
whole group of property with a wide range of uses and occupiers that requires
careful thought as to where it is best sold in order to achieve the best price for
the vendor client.

The value of the lot is not the determining factor, but rather the likely buyer is. Another aspect is the ability of the auctioneer to achieve the appropriate exposure in the market place.

The advantages and disadvantages of location are summarised as follows.

The local and regional auction

- The bidders are based locally or looking locally
- The marketing campaign of the auctioneer will reach all prospective bidders as it can embrace not only local but also national publications, such as *Estates Gazette* and *Country Life*
- The bidders and other local interested parties are unlikely to be prepared to travel any distance
- Proxy or telephone bids are unlikely to be left with an auctioneer that an out-of-town bidder does not know
- The lot is only of local interest
- The lot will be among a large number of other properties and so its uniqueness and individual appeal will tend to be diminished or lost
- With regional collective sales the economies of scale are passed directly down to the individual vendor clients
- Where a bidder is unsuccessful on one lot there is the opportunity to bid on subsequent lots

The London auction

- Accessibility, because London is the single most easily reached location, not only within the U.K. but also from Europe and internationally
- The prestige attracts a wider range of buyers to the sale
- Mailing lists built up over many years of successful collective sales are comprehensive and extensive
- Marketing of a large multi-lot sale achieves the maximum exposure to the market place. Mailing lists extend to thousands and the demand for catalogues ensures a print run of 9000 to 12000
- Advertising is on a national and local basis with the size and spread of advertising of a style and size which it would be difficult for a local firm to match
- The sheer scale of the sale and diversity of the lots attracts wide media interest
- The economies of scale are passed directly down to the individual vendor clients
- Where a bidder is unsuccessful on one lot there is the opportunity to bid on subsequent lots

As can be seen there are compelling reasons for both routes and the auctioneer must weigh up the upside and downside of both options. At the end of the day the best interests of the vendor client are paramount and the decision whether to sell locally or in London has to be reached on a lot by lot basis, coupled with the full agreement of the client. There are many tales of lots being undersold both in London and provincially. The debate will continue as long as there are auctions and in deciding on the route the simple answer is that the best interests of the client must prevail.

Figure 6.1 Advertisement for multi-centre auctions (Courtesy of BR Property, Conrad Ritblat, Hartnell Taylor Cook, and Roy Pugh.)

Private auctions

While auctions are always assumed to be open to anyone who wishes to attend and is able to comply with the auctioneer's conditions for bidding, they have another rarely stated application. This is the private auction which, although little used or understood, is an excellent and extremely fair and reasonable method of resolving a fraught and sensitive situation where, following marketing by private treaty, several parties are offering similar bids for a property. At this point in time, if the agent is not careful, he will be accused on behalf of his client of 'gazumping' and, even with the sealed bid on 'best and highest offer' basis, an unhappy situation will arise with everyone feeling hard done by.

The solution is to halt the negotiations at this stage, to announce that there will be a private auction and immediately to arrange for the vendor's solicitors to draw up a contract and obtain the searches which can be achieved at surprisingly short notice. All the parties are invited to attend at a stated date and time at either the estate agents or solicitors offices. The estate agent will then conduct the proceedings in accordance with the rules of auction, usually starting the bidding at the current offer. The advantage is that everyone involved has the opportunity to see the other parties around the table on an eyeball to eyeball basis with an equal chance to bid on equal terms. Everything is above board and the deal is binding on the fall of the gavel. In the true tradition of auction everything is above board and open for all the participants to see, and they come to the auction to bid on a level playing field. On the fall of the gavel the highest bidder will be bound by the contract and conditions of sale and will sign the memorandum of sale.

7 Marketing Auctions

It will be remembered from the preceding chapters that auction sales, by their very nature, are conducted within a strictly limited time scale. The end result is that the auctioneer must have from the outset a clear, pre-agreed plan for the advertising and media press releases. A great deal of thought and planning must be given to this area of activity at an early stage, usually in parallel with the preparation of the draft auction particulars. Furthermore, the costs of the advertising are usually paid by the vendor client and therefore the auctioneer will need to have quoted accurately for this work and obtained specific approval.

The background

The auctioneer approaches this task keeping in mind the broad choice of marketing options, but essentially this will centre on advertising in the various local, provincial and national newspapers and magazines. However, marketing goes beyond purely advertising in the media and embraces the signboard on the property(ies), posters if used, and press releases to the media, including local and national radio and TV as appropriate. A further indispensable element is the all important mailing lists of applicants and other contacts.

What is the objective of the marketing campaign? The strategy is to generate the maximum amount of interest on the sale day leading to the achievement of the optimum sale price. Usually the auctioneer will be working within a five to eight week time slot between the time that the particulars become available and the auction sale date. A useful tip is to mail out the catalogues or particulars before the first advertisement appears as this will save a lot of duplication, otherwise inevitably applicants on the mailing list will telephone in response to the advertisement on the assumption that they have been overlooked for some reason. The first advertisements are timed to appear at the same time as the auction particulars become available from the printers and the mail shot is sent out.

The vendor clients will be footing the bill and so they will be examining carefully all the costs arising from the marketing of the property. However, if a successful blend of advertising and editorial is achieved this will produce a potent mix, creating maximum market awareness.

Inevitably there is a great temptation to try to advertise too widely and to spread the campaign across a broad range of publications. This can be foolhardy, as the attendant result will be measured by the poor response which in turn will be reflected by a low attendance in the auction room with a correspondingly weak, or even non- existent level of bidding.

Some major auction houses retain specialist marketing consultants, but for most auctioneers the organisation of the sale is undertaken on an in-house basis and the skill of framing up the marketing campaign is based on hard-won experience. The challenge is to identify those media publications that are widely read by both the known *and* potential bidders. Remember that the marketing campaign not only embraces the advertising but also through press releases hopefully editorial and sometimes local and national radio and television interviews. An editorial which is free will frequently achieve a far higher response rate when compared with an advertisement in the same publication. The public tend to read editorial but only at best skim through the advertising section, so the end result is an additional entirely fresh group of applicants. However, always remember that the genuine applicant who is new to the market place will carefully read all the advertisements relative to the type of property which they are seeking and so advertisements are a key element in the marketing of action lots.

Advertisements and press releases have to comply with the law and so must be both accurate and factual in every respect. Photographs, artist's impressions, rents, areas, uses, planning consents and the accommodation are all potential areas for misdescription. The simple rule is to check for accuracy and then check again!

There are six distinct areas of marketing and these tend to overlap and intertwine.

- Advertising in the press and journals
- Editorials in the press and journals
- Television and the radio
- Mailing list and personal contacts
- For Sale boards and posters
- Catalogues/Auction Particulars

Advertising in the press and journals

The range of publications available is extremely wide and a glance at any newsstand will give an insight of the choices on offer. The difficulty is identifying the best publications for the sale in hand, especially if this involves an unusual lot or one which is outside the geographical area familiar to the auctioneer.

The national newspapers and journals together with the local and regional newspapers are relatively simple to select. Many newspapers have regular auction sections, but take care that the correct slot is chosen as frequently there are separate residential, commercial and industrial property, fine art, and agricultural features. Again, with daily newspapers check whether or not there are particular types of property advertised on stated weekdays. To achieve the best response it may be better to advertise a commercial lot on the commercial feature day rather than in the weekly auction section where it will be mixed up with the full range of auction activities.

When planning advertisements you need to place yourself in the role of the potential bidders and to ask yourself which sources and publications they are most likely to refer to and how best to reach out to them. The advertising is aimed at attracting bidders and it is definitely not a self-promoting exercise to publicise the auctioneer. Having said that, there are major benefits to be gained from adopting a distinctive and strong house style for both vendor and auctioneer.

It is prudent to build up a collection of the newspapers and journals which are likely to be regularly used for ease of reference as to layout, styles and format of the auction pages. This information bank should be reinforced by analysing responses by reference to specific publications and dates. This means that when enquiries are received the person will be asked where they saw the advertisement or with more sophisticated systems this can be picked up by use of dedicated telephone lines or the like. Over a period of time a detailed picture can be built up as to the worth of specific publications.

A problem when using the specialist magazines is that they usually have very long copy dates and the timescale of the sale may not permit their use. Always check carefully with them before submitting copy. Watch out for the actual date that the magazine appears on the bookstalls as there is no point in the advertisement producing a flood of enquiries two days before the sale date! A tale which contradicts this comment relates to a small period village house which was advertised in *Country Life* magazine 6 weeks before an auction. On the morning of the sale day a frantic telephone call was received at the auctioneer's office from an applicant. It transpired that the applicant had sold his business in the home counties, completing the deal that morning. To celebrate he and his wife had decided to dine out that night and so she had gone to her hairdressers. Whilst waiting for her appointment she had leafed through a back issue of *Country Life* and spotted the auction advertisement. Amazingly the couple travelled down to the west country, viewed the house late that afternoon and successfully purchased it at auction that evening!

Editorials in the press and journals

The old adage that a picture is worth a thousand words when dealing with 'editorials' can be turned around to a few lines of editorial can be worth many hundreds of pounds spent on advertising. The editorial exposes the property to a vastly wider market place and it will attract enquiries from those who do not necessarily look at the property advertisement section. As an aside it will help dramatically to promote the auctioneer in that niche market and, once the auctioneer becomes known to be active in a particular section, editors will frequently turn to them for comment and input on the auction and property scene even when their own properties are not involved.

A completely different range of people read editorial and newspaper stories as compared with advertisements. Through the editorial stories the net is cast far wider, thus bringing the lot to the notice of many people who otherwise would not have expressed even a passing interest in it.

Journalists are the same as everyone else and inevitably the press release will be skimmed through to establish its provenance and value to the publication. A rambling poorly constructed two page handout will usually end up in the waste paper basket.

Achieving editorial in newspapers and magazines is always a challenge and whilst the very fact that the content centres around an auction is a major plus point, imagination is the key ingredient to success. With an auction there are several approaches to examine:

1. **The Property**
   What is different about this lot?
   Does it have some special connection with the locality?
   Has it featured in the media recently?

2. **The Vendor**
   Can the vendor's name be used?
   Is the vendor known in some other context?

3. **The Price Guide**
   Is there a good story line here?

4. **The reason for an auction**
   Often there is a story on why the lot has come to the auction room.

5. **The market place**
   Is there a comment on supply and demand or interest rates that can be included?
   Can the article be tied into a recent press article or story on the radio or television?

Press releases must therefore be simple, to the point, contain a story line that catches the eye and have a contact name and telephone number for any additional information that the journalist may need. Only include a photograph if it has something to say and catches the eye. Simple pointers include heading the press release 'Press Release' and keeping it to one side of A4 only. Whoever is named as the the contact must be instantly available and also be someone who is articulate. Of course all press releases must be cleared with the vendor client, for once dispatched it is impossible to retract the release.

Media contact list

After a press release has been prepared the auctioneer will circulate it to named journalist and media contacts. The task of maintaining this vital mailing list is difficult as the names always seem to be changing! Finally always attach a copy of the auction particulars to the Press Release.

Television and radio

Local television and radio often pick up on press releases where properties of interest come on to the market, if the press release is tied in to a current news story, or especially where the owner or occupier is well known. Usually an interview with the auctioneer will be incorporated if it is on television and the best location for the interview is in front of the 'For Sale' board.

As an illustration of the effectiveness of achieving a successful press release, a provincial auctioneer was instructed to sell by auction an old derelict Victorian country railway station. A suitable press release was prepared and sent out to newspapers and journals, as well as to the local radio and television stations. The resultant number of column inches of editorial which appeared in a wide range of newspapers stunned the auctioneers who were faced with not one but two reprints of the auction particulars, such was the increased level of enquiry! Close on the heels of this avalanche there followed a regional television interview at the property which in turn led to a national slot the following day. This resulted in a third reprint!

The story did not end there, for on the afternoon of the auction a telephone call came in to the auctioneer's offices from the landlord of the nearby market town hotel to say that people were queuing outside at 5 pm and that usually he did not open his doors until 6 pm. Also, what should he do about the two television crews, complete with cameras and floodlights, as they wanted to set up in the ballroom for the auction sale? Such is the power of a successful press release and the attendant mayhem that the auctioneer must cope with over and above conducting an orderly sale!

Mailing lists and personal contacts

Essential to all successful agency operations and especially auctions is an up-to-date mailing list. For the major auction houses the mail shot for a large collective auction will run at around 10,000. By contrast a local auction of a single lot may only involve a mail shot of 150. Whatever the number the end result of a successful auction is what matters. It is the quality of the mailing list which is so important; an extensive list which only contains a small proportion of genuinely interested names wastes time and resources.

For auctions it is sensible to maintain on the mailing list the names of agents, including contact names rather than merely the firm. They are not in competition with the auctioneer and may well have potential bidders on their books for whom they can act. For the auctioneer coming on to the rostrum to be faced with the sight of familiar agents in the room is welcome, since usually they will be attending on behalf of clients who have instructed them to bid on their behalf.

Similarly, lists should be kept of solicitors, accountants and architects, together with major employers, distributors and retailers. All in all, the broader the base of the list, the better so long as it is maintained on a current footing by continuous updating.

For Sale boards and posters

The old friend, 'the silent salesman', in the shape of the sale board is an important element when marketing property by auction. It spreads the news locally and catches the eye of the passing traffic. When erecting specialised 'one off' boards, always make certain that the planning and bye-law regulations are met and that the appropriate insurance cover is in place. Do not cobble up a standard private treaty board as this will look amateurish and it will fail to convey the message of an auction.

The auction poster is rarely used today, but again it can play a useful role in marketing. The reason for its demise has been the cost of production for relatively short print runs. However, its display in solicitor's offices, at the property and the auction venue all go towards generating interest from untapped sources. Also, it spreads the name of the auctioneer in the quest to establish a niche market.

Catalogues/Auction particulars

As mentioned earlier a strong and individual house style, a logical format for the presentation of the information and accuracy of content will not only enhance the reputation of the auctioneer but also ensure a regular following of potential buyers.

A comparison of present-day catalogues with those of two decades ago, clearly demonstrates that important changes have evolved over the years, especially in the field of collective auctions. The emphasis of providing every practical assistance for would-be bidders is achieved through printing Proxy Bidding authorities, help lines and helpful 'do's and don'ts', together with useful hints on attending auction sales.

Advertising

From the foregoing remarks it will be seen that whether dealing with a single lot or larger collective auction sale the plan of campaign for the marketing has to be approached by drawing on the experiences of previous auctions and always remembering the short timescale. Four factors which will be taken into account are:

- The value of the lot/sale
- The appeal of the lot/sale
- The likely type of bidder
- Copy deadlines and publication dates of newspapers and magazines

The value of the lot/sale
Working on the assumed sale price, the size and number of advertisements can be assessed. The advantage of the collective auction is that there are important cost savings because much of the information together with the auctioneer's name and house style only appears once and does not have to be repeated for each lot.

The appeal of the lot/sale
Consider the lot(s) and their appeal through the eyes of the potential bidders and where they might look in the newspapers and media for news that this lot(s) is on the market. Will an industrial buyer read the same publication as a retailer, or an owner occupier read the same newspaper as a farmer? Likewise how do you reach the agents and scouts of whom there are many, who act as conduits feeding through to specific clients' properties that are on the market?

The likely type of bidder
To a degree this overlaps with the last paragraph, but here we are looking at marketing from the standpoint of the bidder rather than the property. Investment lots, especially of a mixed use, a lot with part vacant possession and national versus local interest lots are all examples where bidders may come from more than one specific source. In recent years the classic case is the repossessed home sold in a major collective sale where the successful buyer at auction may be a local owner occupier or equally a dealer.

This means that the auction sale has to be advertised both nationally and locally.

Copy deadlines and publication dates of newspapers and magazines
All publications work to strict deadlines and advertising has to be geared around them. Plenty of lead-in time must be allowed and actual publication dates for specialist magazines must be watched. There is no point in taking advertising

space in a journal which appears on the bookstalls only a short time before the auction.

Advertising is a fascinating subject in its own right. Accepting that the agent's role is to sell the property at the best price the agent in selecting the various newspapers must balance cost against circulation with the object of maximising the budget. Most auctioneers will monitor the response, identifying the source of each reply, and thus assessing the worth of each publication.

This is an essential element of research when weighing up the options which are available and advising your vendor client.

It is too easy to fall into the trap of styling the advertisement to promote the name of the firm rather than the property and likewise to use a publication which is not best suited to the property but is one where the firm regularly appears.

The question 'How do we reach the largest market place within the budget?' is the key to selecting publications and often has to be balanced as between national and local newspapers. In part this will be determined by the policy of the auctioneer's firm, but whatever the pattern of advertising it is essential that this is reviewed on a routine basis. Fragmentation of the advertising programme is another pitfall. Insertions which are placed throughout a large range of publications in the hope that at least one will catch the eye of bidders are both a waste of your client's money and unproductive. Always think through carefully the advertising campaign and build it up on the strength of previous responses to particular publications.

8 Events Prior to the Auction

Unlike private treaty sales, an auction sale to a degree runs under its own momentum and all those involved in the auction team are carried along, hopefully imbued with a strong sense of urgency. This sense of urgency is triggered by the fact that there is an exceptionally tight time-frame within which the lot is marketed and potential bidders are found. Inevitably, would-be buyers will wish to inspect the lot in which they are interested several times; then there will be a whole host of questions arising from these inspections; and, once surveyors, valuers and solicitors for the buyers are involved, yet more queries will be raised. All these have to be answered as quickly as possible. Alongside this activity the auctioneer will be busy trouble-shooting all the multitude of problems which might spring out of the woodwork. Truly in this theatre time is of the essence!

The timescale

For each type of auction sale the timescale will vary to some degree, but broadly the framework is as follows:

Week 1.   Acceptance of instructions and initial inspection, followed by preparation of draft particulars.
- Terms of appointment sent to the vendor client.
- With collective sales, the terms and conditions of appointment are required to be approved and signed by the vendor client before the auction house proceeds with the instruction, which is a step ahead of most local auctioneers.
- In the case of regular contributors to collective sales, major auction houses will often handle these instructions on a rolling programme, and not issue separate terms and conditions for each lot.

Week 2.   Vendor client confirms acceptance of auctioneer's appointment, not in the case of the main auction houses – see above – but is usually the case with local auctioneers.
- Vendor client instructs solicitors.
- Auctioneer confirms in writing the reservation of the sale venue and that the necessary insurance cover together with fire regulations and any other local authority regulations are current.
- Auctioneer writes to the solicitors requesting copies of all the relevant information relating to the property including copies of conveyance or lease

plans. This enables the auctioneer to check on the boundaries and extent of the property.

- The auctioneer will also ask the solicitor to undertake the searches and for the vendor to complete the enquiries on contract.
- Completion of enquiries, circulation of draft particulars to the vendor client and solicitors.
- Preparation of marketing plan and budget and circulation to the vendor client.
- When a Buyer's Pack is to be provided, a surveyor will be instructed to undertake a RICS/ISVA Homebuyer Survey, but this will not contain any reference to value.

Week 3. Approval of draft particulars, confirmation of content and submission to printers.

- Approval by the vendor client of the marketing plan and budget.
- Solicitor sends draft General and Special Conditions of Sale for checking and approval.
- Signwriter instructed.

Week 4. Advertising plan activated.

- Auction 'For Sale' board erected.
- Auction particulars circulated to vendor client, solicitors, auction venue and mailing list.
- Press releases sent out.
- Solicitors send the General and Special Conditions of Sale together with other relevant documents to be held on the auction file.

Week 5. Viewing commences in earnest.

- Response to advertisements and issuing of particulars to enquirers.
- It is in the second week of advertising that the peak level of enquiries is achieved.

Week 6. Pre-auction offers begin to be received.

- End of main thrust of advertising programme.
- Fresh Press release sent out.
- For collective sales a seminar may be arranged for the auctioneer and the solicitors to explain the procedures, how to bid, and legal formalities to potential bidders who are not familiar with auctions.

Week 7. The lotting and order of sale reviewed.

- Reserve price discussed and agreed with vendor client.
- Final check made with the solicitors over any last minute queries which may have arisen.
- Auction Addenda if required circulated with the Auction Reminder.

- Auction Reminder sent to all those who have received the auction particulars, mailing list and the general enquiries.
- Venue reservation re-checked if an acknowledgement has not been received.
- If solicitors are attending the sale, they are reminded of sale date, time and venue.

Week 8.   Auction Addenda checked for detailed accuracy.
- Rostrum announcements prepared.

Each auction sale will have the timescale tailored to its own unique requirements, but whether it is shortened to 5 weeks or extended to 12 weeks the one certainty is that there will be a strict end date, namely the auction. The workload of the various sections will be telescoped or extended but the overall pattern remains the same.

The way in which the auction file is constructed and the checks incorporated in it are critical to the success of a smooth path to the rostrum. While every office today will have standard procedures and systems to be followed to comply with 'best practice' and the legal requirements when following the private treaty route, auction sales and their files must embrace all these aspects under one central reference source. This is essential as the auction team need to have access to one reference point for all aspects of the latest state of play as the auction proceeds from the initial instruction through to the sale date.

Computer systems are common-place in offices today, but for most firms they will not entirely replace the hard copy file. Those handling collective sales rely on the latest technology to help them meet the deadlines associated with generating and completing the auction catalogue through to the completion of the sales, monitoring every step along the way through use of the latest software packages.

Matters occurring during this period

The General and Special Conditions of Sale

The question as to whether or not the General and Special Conditions of Sale together with the Memorandum of Sale are printed in the auction particulars was discussed in Chapter 4. If they are to be included, the optimum notice of the decision to go to auction must be given to the solicitors and sufficient time allowed in the timetable before going into print.

It is for this reason and also cost that for individual lot auctions these are usually left out and made available for inspection at the offices of the auctioneer and solicitor. Where applicants ask for copies of them and other relevant legal documents it is recommended that they are provided by the solicitor rather than by the auctioneer. This ensures that the applicant receives the latest and most accurate version and so avoids any slip-ups.

Viewing

Many agents are concerned about coping with the increased office traffic, both visitors and telephone enquiries, that an auction will generate. Delegated staff need to be briefed to handle the auction which will ease the situation. For lots which are likely to attract overwhelming interest the vendor client should be warned in advance and suitable arrangements made. In some cases the answer might be to adopt the 'open house' viewing with stated times when access can be obtained. This type of viewing helps to underline the sense of urgency of an auction to all parties and the strength of the interest.

The peak time for viewings is usually in the second and third week following the circulation of particulars and the commencement of the advertising programme.

Handling offers prior to the auction

Most seasoned auctioneers are of the view that once a decision has been made to take a property to auction, then under only very limited circumstances can a lot be sold before the auction. However, there can be no hard and fast rule on this subject, as so many factors come into play. Some key points to consider are:

(a) Are the General and Special Conditions of Sale, Memorandum and Searches available?

In the event of a decision to sell being made, these documents must be available. It is essential that both the vendor and purchaser can be bound by signing the Memorandum of Sale attaching to the documents. This is why they have to be available at the moment that the auction particulars are circulated.

(b) Has the right to sell prior to the auction been reserved?

This right on behalf of the vendor client must be stated on the auction particulars. Furthermore, a point sometimes overlooked by the auctioneer is that they should make it clear there is always the possibility of a sale before the auction. Advertisements should also state the fact in order to avoid any misunderstanding.

Each auction house has its own form and wording of the agency contract and a totally separate letter of instruction would be required if a sale prior to auction was contemplated.

(c) How long has the lot been on the market?

The offer which is made in the first week of marketing may be a tactical move to secure a purchase at a reasonable price before the lot is exposed to the full force of the market place. Be prepared to answer the question from the vendor 'Has the market been fully tested?'

Always be on guard against falling into the trap of creating an auction before an auction! The initial reaction to an offer above the top limit of the guide price may be to accept it and this may well be the attitude of the vendor client. Remember that they are probably not familiar with the ways of the property market and will need firm and positive guidance from the auctioneer.

Keep to the forefront of your mind the basic underlying reasons for taking the lot to auction. Pose the question as to whether or not a sale prior to the auction will achieve the optimum price.

(d) How close is the auction date?

Most auctioneers follow the rule that there is a point in time after which the lot cannot be sold prior to the auction. This is to allow sufficient time to contact all potential bidders either personally, through advertising, or by post.

However, there is nothing to prevent a sale being agreed and contracts exchanged right up to the moment that the auctioneer reaches that lot in the catalogue. It is not unknown for the auctioneer to be handed a list of withdrawn lots immediately before commencing the auction.

Apart from the embarrassment that this action creates for the auctioneer, the awkward fact is that inevitably there will be bidders present who have spent time and money on placing themselves in a position to be able to bid and, to put it mildly, they will not be pleased! In the unlikely event of lots being regularly withdrawn from sales, the auctioneer needs to be on guard against upsetting the hardcore of speculator and investor bidders that attend his sales.

Local and regional auctioneers tend towards the view that there is a cut-off point about seven to ten days before the sale date after which, unless there are extremely strong reasons to the contrary, the lot must go through the auction room.

(e) Have the legal documents been inspected?

As a first step, before going into the procedure of discussing the offer with the vendor client and other interested parties, always check up with the solicitors as to whether or not the party has inspected the legal documentation.

It is a useless and time consuming exercise to start the hare running over a possible prior sale if the bidder is likely to raise questions and difficulties over the contract. Without question in these circumstances the offer should be declined, and the lot offered at auction.

(f) Has a survey/mortgage valuation/engineer's report been made?

Similar comments apply here as in paragraph (e) above.

(g) What is the vendor client's position and attitude?

Just because the right to sell before the auction has been reserved, this does not mean that it has to be exercised. Some vendor clients will prefer that the lot is offered at auction so that their duty is discharged. For example executors, trustees, and where there are conflicting interests.

On the other hand the vendor client may be anxious to have the certainty of the cash in the bank and this can a sound reason for a prior sale.

Equally, the vendor client may be non-committal as to which course of action to follow and here the auctioneer will have to bring all his knowledge and skills into play to achieve the right decision. Each time this situation arises is unique and experience has shown that, if in doubt, then continue to proceed to auction. The strength of interest in the lot is an important factor, and given that there is more than one party, then the prudent course is to go to auction.

(h) What is the level of interest?

The in-house office systems will show at a glance the number of viewings and resultant interest. This will influence the advice which will be given, since when there has been a high level of interest, several surveys undertaken and a number of parties indicating that they will be attending the auction, backed up by the solicitors reporting various approaches for documentation, the fact is that the auctioneer will have to consult with a large number of potential bidders.

Given these circumstances the danger is of entering into the familiar scenario of the private auction before the public auction! Again, if in doubt, then proceed to auction.

(i) Are there any other conditions attaching to the offer?

Sometimes a pre-auction offer will be subject to conditions seeking to vary the Special Conditions or imposing new conditions. Whatever the terms are, they will need to be examined carefully and taken into account in determining the course of action. The difficulty arises in weighing the value of the offer against others made strictly in accordance with the Special Conditions of Sale.

As will be gathered from these headings there is no hard and fast rule on when to accept an offer prior to the auction. However, when a substantial offer is made which the auctioneer considers is unlikely to be matched by anyone else, then this offer may be carefully considered provided that it passes all the criteria. The next step is to go to all the other interested bidders, often difficult to identify, and state that a bid has been received and that serious thought is being given to a sale prior to the auction. This is not a sealed bid situation and must be stressed as such, since the genuine intent is to determine whether or not anyone will equal or better the offer. In either case, if the response is positive there are sound reasons to continue with the auction.

As a general rule the auctioneer will not disclose the amount of the offer, rather that it is substantial having regard to the Price Guide.

Assuming that all these hurdles have been crossed and a decision has been taken to sell before the auction, then the auctioneer has to achieve both an exchange of contracts and clearance of the deposit cheque; not until then, and only at that point, can the lot be withdrawn from the auction, as it has been sold.

Procedure where lots are sold prior to auction

With the lot withdrawn, the file and mailing list must be combed through so that every enquiry for auction particulars on that lot is notified. There is nothing worse than a potential bidder turning up at the sale venue only to discover that the lot has been withdrawn. The auctioneer's reputation and standing with valuable buyers can suffer irreparable damage in these circumstances.

Attitude to bids prior to auction

Auctioneers adopt different approaches to offers prior to the auction. The first is to encourage actively bids prior to the sale on the basis that these assist towards both adjusting the Price Guide and advising on the reserve price for the auction.

The second is to deter bids prior to the sale on the basis that the fundamental decision at the outset was to take the lot to auction. Indeed, this may have been the specific instruction of the vendor client. However, under current legislation, whenever a bid is received it has to be reported to the client.

As a parting shot on the subject, this is a highly contentious area. One question always in the back of the auctioneer's mind is whether or not the office systems have successfully recorded all the interested parties and what about the rank outsider of whom there is no record.

Auctioneers accept that, no matter how efficient the office systems are, there is always the strong likelihood over the span of several sales that the successful buyer will be unknown. This can occur for several reasons; they can be acting through a third party, they have slipped through the office systems, or they have deliberately maintained a low profile.

To try and reduce the possibility of this situation arising many auctioneers include in their 'General Remarks' a clause to the effect that anyone interested must register this fact with the auctioneers.

In conclusion, this niggling element is not dampened by the long established fact that most pre-auction bidders, in spite of their protestations to the contrary, attend at the auction sale and actively bid!

The Price Guide

While the general approach is for auctioneers to give price guides, this practice is not universal. With all the major collective sales catalogues there will be printed, or more usually enclosed, a schedule giving price guides for each lot. Conversely, others will put forward the case for not stating any figures, on the basis that bidders must take their own advice and counsel.

The case for providing price guides is that it assists applicants and stimulates interest, thus leading to a more successful outcome in the auction room. Certainly, over recent years with the marked shift in attitudes and legislation towards consumer protection, the use of and approach to the price guide has altered dramatically.

Historically, the price guide was used to stimulate interest by deliberately understating the figure and then gradually increasing it once interest was established. Today, this practice must no longer be used as current law regards it as misleading and deceitful.

In today's market the Price Guide has to be set at a realistic level based on market research. Prospective purchasers must have no grounds to complain that they have been misled and as the timescale proceeds towards the sale date, the figure ought to be revised to reflect the interest and offers received. Usually the guide is expressed as a bracket of figures spanning the anticipated price. The span will be narrow at the lower level of values and correspondingly higher as these increase. The objective of the Price Guide is to generate the maximum interest in the lot and to encourage those interested to follow through the steps to enable them to bid on the sale day.

The Price Guide must be realistic, be capable of being shown to have a close relationship to the reserve, and whenever possible be adjusted to reflect the latest situation as time ticks by towards the auction.

These prices are for guide purposes only and may or may not reflect the selling price.
These are also subject to change.

B R PROPERTY BOARD AUCTION

WEDNESDAY 26TH FEBRUARY 1997
MANCHESTER AIRPORT, TERMINAL 2
COMMENCING AT 2.30PM

<u>**SUMMARY OF LOTS**</u>

Auctioneers
Property Consultants
Surveyors
Valuers

LOT	PROPERTY	GUIDE PRICE
1	Car Park, Bridge Road, West Kirby	£25–£30,000
2	Former Goods Yard, Chatburn, nr Clitheroe	£1–£1,500
3	Lion Street, Oakengates, Telford	£19–£22,000
4	Beach Road, Barmouth, North Wales	£26–£29,000
5	Premises, Station Road, Pannal, nr Harrogate	£45–£50,000
6	Land, Pontefract Lane, Leeds	£2–£3,000
7	Land adj River Brock, Brock nr Garstang	Without Reserve
8	Land Whalley, Lancashire	Without Reserve
9	B.R.S.A Club, Tibshelf Road, Westhouses	£32–£42,000
10	Agricultural Land, Castle Donnington	£18–£22,000
11	Station Road, Sowerby Bridge, West Yorks	£35–£40,000
12	Former Goods Yard, Burton Salmon, nr Ferrybridge	£2–£3,000
13	Former Goods Yard, Capenhurst, Wirral	£18–£20,000
14	Land, Atherton Way, Atherton, Lancs	£3–£5,000
15	Land, Former Briedden Station, Middletown, Montgomery	£8–£12,000
16	Land, Post Lane, Endon, Staffordshire	£2–£3,000
17	Land, Midland Terrace, Frizinghall, Bradford	£14–£16,000
18	Land, Rowms Lane, Swinton, Rotherham	£18–£20,000
19	Land Warrington Road, Platt Bridge, nr Wigan	£2–£3,000
20	Land/Pond, Moss Lane, Croston, nr Chorley	Without Reserve
21	Land, Spa Well Lane, Croston, nr Chorley	Without Reserve
22	Former Station House, Caersws, Montgomery	£18–£22,000
23	2 Parcels of Land off A458, Buttington, Welshpool	£4–£6,000
24	Land Britannia Rd, Bishopton Rd, Stockton–on–Tees	£25–£28,000
25	Land, West Carr Road, Retford, Notts	£30–£35,000
26	Land, Ravenhead, St Helens	£2–£3,000
27	Land, Jackson Street, Birkenhead	£10–£15,000
28	Land, Bow Street, nr Aberystwyth	£3–£5,000
29	The Station Inn, Porthmadog	£52,500–£57,500
30	Land and Buildings, Weddington Terrace, Nuneaton	£30–£35,000
31	Land, Burgar Road, Thorne South, nr Doncaster	£2–£3,000
32	Fishing Ponds, Thorne North, nr Doncaster	£2–£3,000
33	Land, South of Station, Thorne South, nr Doncaster	£500–£1000
34	Land, Former Goods Yard, Thorne South, nr Doncaster	£3–£5,000
35	Land, Darnall, Sheffield	£15–£20,000
36	Land near Manchester Road, Northwich, Cheshire	£7–£9,000
37	Shop Premises & Garages, Hucknall Lane, Nottingham	£20–£24,000
38	Post Office, Hucknall Lane, Nottingham	£35–£38,000
39	Compound adj to Longton Station, Stoke on Trent	£20–£23,000

11 Cross Street,
Preston PR1 3LT
Tel: (01772) 883399
Fax: (01772) 883377

Figure 8.1 Example of a list of lots for auction with price guide. Note some are
'without reserve'. (Courtesy of the Roy Pugh Company)

Updated Press Releases

Whether or not the original Press Release has been well received by the media there is a second opportunity to gain further coverage if a suitable story emerges during the marketing of the property. This may hinge on a massive response, a change in planning circumstances, something coming to light such as an unexpected historical link or someone flying halfway around the world to view. Imagination is the key and it is amazing how with a run-of-the-mill lot something can appear on the scene to provide copy for a good news story.

The Addendum

If in the course of marketing any alterations are made to the particulars and the information relating to the lot, then it will be necessary to issue an Addendum. This will be circulated to everyone who has received the particulars and if it affects the accuracy of the copy in the advertisements, then these will also have to be amended. The timing of the circulation of the Addendum will depend upon when the auctioneer became aware of the amendments. Whether or not the Addendum has been circulated, it must be made available to everyone who attends at the sale and its content explained to all telephone bidders. For other proxy bidders who have left bids with the auctioneer the disclosure of its content will depend upon the wording of the authority which was signed by the bidders.

9 Setting the Reserve

In essence the success or failure of an auction hinges on setting the reserve price at the correct figure. In Chapter 2 reference was made to establishing at the outset whether or not the vendor client was of the same mind as the auctioneer in respect of the realisation price. Put simply, if there was a major divergence of opinion at that stage, then the auctioneer must resolve the issue there and then, otherwise potential disaster hovers in the wings!

The tendency to follow the simple route of merely adopting the reserve price which was suggested at the outset is not only foolhardy but also fails abysmally in the duty of care to the vendor client. The whole objective of the auction is to achieve the optimum sale price under the hammer in the room, and in reaching this target the reserve plays a vital role. Do not confuse the Reserve Price with the actual sale price, for the two figures may often be quite different.

Factors to take into account when advising on the Reserve

The setting of the reserve price is rarely simple and the complex route to agreement requires a great deal of understanding and care with many factors to be taken into account. An auctioneer will usually take on board all or some of the following elements when advising on the reserve price:

Active interest

- The number of people who have inspected the lot.
- How many of these have been for a second or subsequent time?

Office and auction file records play a vital part here and provide an essential information base for discussions with the vendor client.

Survey, mortgage valuation, and structural survey

Which firms have carried these out and, of equal importance, for whom? The latter point is vital as it helps to pinpoint the potential bidders when aligned alongside other information and goes together to build up the overall picture.

Bear in mind that the word 'survey' encompasses a wide range of reports, including structural survey, detailed building survey, in-depth building survey and valuation for mortgage/loan purposes.

Whenever possible the auctioneer's negotiator needs to elicit from the surveyor/valuer after the inspection any comments on structural condition, costings, and value. Again these are vital elements towards determining the relative level of value and reserve.

Offers submitted prior to auction

Today, every office must have a specific system in place for recording and reporting offers. The record must not only note such details as name, address, and contact telephone number, but also the date and time together with the offer and any conditions attaching to it.

Also the record will note the name of the person receiving the offer and the action route that is taken subsequently, again including dates.

When examining the offers, it goes without saying that each one must be assessed as to the ability of the offeror, not only to sign a binding contract and pay the deposit, but also to complete on the due date. This aspect has already been examined in depth within Chapter 8.

In formulating your advice to the vendor client the pattern of offers, the strength, the keenness to acquire, and side issues thrown up need to be carefully weighed up. Usually the vendor client will merely latch on to the figure and ignore the other factors.

The market place

All the foregoing factors are important and have to be taken into account along with the strengths and weaknesses of the market place. Your office must be closely in touch with the market sector in which the lot lies. For example, if the office usually handles commercial and residential, then if the lot is a filling station how strong is your information base in this specialist sector?

Circumstances can change quickly, influencing vendors and purchasers as to their perceived level of values. Interest rates, planning, and the political scene are but three elements in the complex web that comes together to create the level of demand and willingness to buy. Do not overlook the key factors of supply and demand.

The reason for selling

For every lot the auctioneer must examine the underlying reasons why they are being brought forward for auction. Perhaps it is to clear a deceased's estate or the result of a change in investment policy within a property portfolio. Whatever the reason, this will influence the approach to setting the reserve. This may range from the need to raise funds to merely a desire to test the market.

Timescale for fixing and recording the Reserve

Now that the basic and underlying elements for advising on the reserve have been identified, there is another essential ingredient to take on board, namely the timescale which operates between the auctioneer advising on reserve and the actual auction sale date.

Auctioneers of collective sales tend to agree the reserve at the outset of the instruction and this pattern is increasingly common today. However, for some vendor clients the reserve will be fixed towards the end of, or at the end of, the marketing programme. On the one hand the advice may be needed in writing several weeks before the the auction date, and on the other the actual reserve may be settled in the room immediately before the start of the sale.

With major collective sales, as a general rule where the reserve prices have not been agreed at the outset, they are agreed during the week preceding the sale date.

The parameters for the reserve or the actual reserve price must be agreed with the vendor client at the outset because there must be a genuine relationship between the Price Guide and the reserve. The latter is then tested against the former during the marketing and the one adjusted against the other. The relationship must be maintained for if the reserve at any time can be shown to have been outside the range of the Price Guide, then it is likely that a misleading statement has been made under the Property Misdescriptions Act 1991.

Whatever the timescale, the auctioneer must have the reserve price confirmed in writing on the auction file before offering the lot. Each firm will have its own form and style of wording. The reason for a written file record is simply that it protects all parties in the event of a dispute after the sale, especially where the lot is sold on the reserve, or where there is active bidding but it is withdrawn when the reserve price is not reached.

To reach the stage of confirming the reserve price the auctioneer will have either made an appointment with the vendor client to discuss in depth his reasoning and advice as to the reserve, taking all the factors into account, or he will have written a letter about it. In the latter instance the letter needs to be laid out clearly, preferably under logical orderly headings, clearly reasoned, and with a concluding positive recommendation.

Whether the auctioneer arranges a meeting at the office or the vendor client's home, preparation is the key to a successful outcome. As with any meeting, allow sufficient time and appreciate that an elderly couple selling their home may require more explanation and background, including how the actual auction takes place, as compared with the director of a company. In the former case reassurance is the key and in the latter all that is required are straightforward facts.

Extraneous factors relating to the Reserve

Life is such that not all bidders make life simple for the poor auctioneer! Regularly, bidders will lie low and not disclose their interest, working through third party agents and this is where careful recording of all enquiries and viewings sometimes, but not always, may help to identify them. Indeed, it is a familiar tale of auctioneers where a keenly sought after lot will be sold in the room to a completely unknown bidder. Not all buyers will even become known at the fall of the hammer, as they will work through third party nominees or agents.

When weighing up all the factors in order to advise the vendor client, the auctioneer must balance up the detailed knowledge of the market place in its broadest sense, along with the factual information on the file embracing those who have viewed, submitted offers, and made enquiries through the vendor's solicitors.

Remember that the reserve price is the figure below which the auctioneer cannot sell. The success or failure of the auction crucially relies on the figure at which the reserve price is fixed. Often to the outsider it is not appreciated that the relation of the reserve to the actual sale price is such that if the reserve is pitched at the right level, then a higher sale price can be achieved through competitive bidding.

As an example, say the reserve price is set at £77,500 in the hope that based on the in-house information a known bidder might go up to that figure. This happens and there is a pregnant silence with no reaction, the auctioneer is on the reserve and apparently no more bids to come in the room! Upon the auctioneer stating that 'the property is in the room' or some such well worn phrase to show that the lot will be sold, then surprise, surprise, someone else starts bidding! Perhaps another party will enter the affray and the end result is a final sale price under the hammer of £81,600. In this example a figure of £1600 was achieved above the comparative market value, and £4100 above the Reserve Price.

At the post mortem back in the office, closer examination of the file shows that the vendor client's solicitors had not one but three enquiries on the contract and conditions of sale. Everyone was so wrapped up in the known bidder and the fact that an offer had been submitted, that they had overlooked this important factor, namely enquiries of the vendor's solicitors.

Incidentally, the practice of the manner by which the auctioneer discloses to those in the room that the bidding for a lot has reached or exceeded the reserve and will be sold varies widely throughout the country. Many consider that it is not good practice to state the fact and others remain silent on this point until there is a lull in the bidding once the reserve is passed.

The duty of care and a genuine professional approach when discussing and advising on the reserve to the client cannot be stressed too strongly. Over the years experience has shown that not only the private vendor but also the trustee, executor and the like may tend to rely on the auctioneer. Never assume that, just because a client apparently has some knowledge of property matters, any lesser level of advice and care is due.

Naturally, there is the strong desire to achieve a sale in the room for obvious reasons, but against this force must be set the overriding objective of disposing of the lot at the best price. The experience of the auctioneer and the team handling the sale must all be drawn together and out of their combined knowledge is distilled the recommended reserve price at auction. The advice needs to be arrived at after careful and thoughtful discussion in the office, involving all the team concerned with the sale. Under no circumstances should the advice be a last minute affair, given in 'the hurly burly' of the last moments before the sale commences as inevitably those moments will be full of interruptions and tension. Where decisions are to be made at this late stage it is best either to have a separate room set aside for such meetings, or for the rural one lot public house sale to retire to the auctioneer's car, away from flapping ears!

Recording the Reserve

Once the reserve is agreed with the vendor client the immediate problem is how to keep this figure as strictly confidential between the parties. The auctioneer is under the clear duty to the client to maintain absolute confidentiality as to the reserve price and in an office of any size this can present practical difficulties. A simple solution is to place the note of the reserve in a clearly marked envelope on the file.

In the offices of country auctioneers the old practice of recording the reserve in code is still used. This is a traditional method which becomes second nature to auctioneers and valuers for noting all confidential figures. It uses a ten letter word, for example CHELMSFORD. C equals 1 and so on through to D which equals 0.

Generally, the reserve price is only known to the vendor client, the auctioneer and occasionally the client's solicitor and so it must remain. Later on the auctioneer's clerk once at the rostrum will become privy to the reserve price (see Chapter 13).

Modern practice with collective sales requires every reserve price to be confirmed in writing to the auctioneer. This may be in the form of a letter, in the Agency Contract, or a fax. All the instructions on reserves are held in one 'Reserve File' and also recorded on a schedule for use by the auctioneer and the clerk (see sample form in Figure 9.1). The auctioneer will then check the schedule again against original letters on the file and enter these onto the auction catalogue which will be used on the rostrum.

File Record of the Reserve Price

Messrs ...., auctioneers, of Market Place, Northleach, Glos. are authorised to offer

No. 345 High Street, Cirencester, Glos.

as described in the attached auction catalogue, namely as Lot 23, to be offered in the Collective Sale on 23rd November 1997

(Delete as appropriate)
Subject to a fixed reserve price of..
Subject to a discretionary reserve price of..........................
Subject to the disclosed reserve price of.............................
As an unreserved lot with no reserve price.........................

in the sum of £87,500
(words) Eighty Seven Thousand Five Hundred Pounds

Authorised Signatory.............................
on behalf of...
Dated 20th November 1997.

Figure 9.1 Recording the reserve price

Types of reserve price

There are several expressions of the reserve price and each plays a very different role both in the auction room and within the marketing leading up to the sale day.

The Fixed Reserve Price

This is the usual form of reserve price. As its name infers, it is a stated fixed figure. The majority of auctions are conducted subject to a fixed reserve.

The Disclosed Reserve, otherwise known as the Upset Reserve

Rarely adopted these days, it was a familiar approach in the late 1920s and early 1930s through that period of deep recession. The lot is marketed from the outset with the reserve price clearly stated on all literature and advertising. By expressing an understated figure, say 20% below the mean market value, it is aimed at stimulating optimum interest within the marketing period. It is especially appropriate when offering difficult lots to value, for example the site of a former rural telephone exchange, a disused railway tunnel or a public toilet.

Auctioneers do not favour this approach generally, for the simple reason that from Day 1 the price cannot be reviewed against the reaction of prospective bidders and, once on the rostrum, the only route open is to put the lot up at that figure with no opportunity of stimulating the bidding

However, the use of the Disclosed Reserve is becoming more frequently used and, as Gary Murphy of Allsop & Co said at a lecture, the great benefit of its use is that it stimulates advance interest and as a result the competition in the room is substantially increased, often leading to a higher realisation price under the hammer.

The Discretionary Reserve

Few text books refer to this type of reserve, but some vendor clients ask the auctioneer to conduct the auction on the basis that the reserve is set within a bracket of figures, for example £75,000 to £77,500. Most auctioneers do not favour this form of instruction as it leaves them in an invidious position since they are pitting their wits against the bidder, live in the room. This can often end up in a 'no bid' situation, namely with a genuine bid above the lower reserve but with the auctioneer landing up with the final bid above, and no further bidding. The lot is therefore withdrawn on the basis that the reserve at the higher figure has not been achieved.

The interesting question here, as yet untested in the courts, is whether or not the actual reserve could be said to be the lower figure, and that therefore the bids by the auctioneer above that figure amount to fraud. For this reason most auctioneers are not prepared to accept this type of instruction and always insist that the reserve is fixed at a stated figure.

The Unreserved Sale

While not strictly falling within this category, mention must be made of this important type of instruction as it does arise occasionally. The client may direct that a lot is offered without reserve or the auctioneer may recommend this approach under certain circumstances.

Unlike chattels auctions it is unusual for a real property to be offered for sale at auction without a reserve. Where an auctioneer is instructed to proceed on this basis the vendor client needs to be made aware that there is no safety net and to take the extreme situation the lot could be knocked down on a maiden bid of £1.00!

Usually the decision will be taken at the outset of the marketing of the lot and great play will be made on the fact in all publicity in the hope that dealers and speculators will be attracted to bid for the lot in the anticipation of acquiring a bargain.

An auctioneer faced with an unreserved lot and aware of the fact from the outset can stimulate additional interest by making the fact known in the particulars and the advertising. It will also make excellent copy for a press release.

The reason for offering a lot without reserve is either that the client has instructed the lot to be offered on this basis, or that the auctioneer has advised this course of action. With the latter it may be that the property is almost impossible to value, perhaps an awkward small parcel of land with no planning potential and patently of no identifiable value.

The Semi-Disclosed Reserve

This is another form of reserve which is not often referred to, but it has its uses in the range of options open to the auctioneer when advising the client on the best route to follow. This is simply a variation on the Disclosed Reserve, but unlike the former which states a fixed figure, the latter is expressed by the words 'The Reserve will not exceed £...'. This has the advantage of leaving the door open for the auctioneer to advise the client on fixing the Reserve closer to the sale date, but not above the stated figure as advertised. Assuming that the advertised figure is somewhat below the deemed market value, it has the advantage of stimulating interest and shows a clear intent on the part of the vendor to achieve a sale under the hammer.

The statute law relating to reserve price

As stated at the beginning of Chapter 4 there is relatively little statute law on real property auctions and even less on the Reserve Price.

The 'Guidance Notes for Auctioneers' issued jointly by The Royal Institution of Chartered Surveyors and The Incorporated Society of Valuers & Auctioneers has a specific section on the Reserve Price. Section 2.7 sets out matters relating to the reserve as matters of 'best practice' (see Appendix A).

The Guidance Notes state that 'it is usual for a a reserve price to be fixed prior to auction day. This is the figure below which the Auctioneer is not authorised to sell at auction.

Any reserve price will remain strictly confidential to the Auctioneer, his staff and the vendor and the Auctioneer will not disclose reserve prices to any third parties unless instructed so to do by the vendors. Only with the agreement of the vendor will a reserve price be disclosed in the catalogue or at the auction.

The existence, but not the amount, of the reserve should be disclosed in the General Conditions of Sale with an indication of the Auctioneer's right to bid on behalf of the vendor up to, but not at or above the reserve price.'

On reading through the preceding paragraphs it should be borne in mind that The Guidance Notes are issued on the basis of 'best practice' for professional auctioneers. In the working environment the auctioneer is likely to advise on the reserve and will obtain the written authority of the vendor (see end of chapter). As to disclosure of the reserve the auctioneer will not reveal this to anyone and where there is a disclosed reserve again as stated the authority of the vendor client, preferably in writing, should be obtained prior to stating the figure in the auction catalogue and in advertisements and press releases.

Again the existence, but not under any circumstances the amount, of the figure must be stated in the Conditions of Sale coupled with the auctioneer's right to bid up to the reserve. Note that the auctioneer's right is only to bid up to the reserve but not at the figure. Assuming that only one person is bidding actively and that the reserve price is £50,000, the auctioneer will step the last bids (regulating the bidding and increments) so that a genuine bid from those present in the sale room is made at £50,000. His last bid will be therefore at £49,000 or £49,500 depending on whether the bids are being taken in £1000 or £500 units. The result is that the genuine bid will be made at £50,000 which is on the reserve, and so the property will be sold unless further genuine bidding ensues.

The Sale of Land by Auction Act 1867 became known as the 'Puffers Act'. This phrase referred to the practice of auctioneers and their client bidding at the sale and so introducing secret bidding into the proceedings.

As John Murdoch states in *Law of Estate Agency and Auctions* (1994), the overall effect of the Act appears to be as follows in respect of the Reserve Price:

1. A puffer (including the auctioneer) may not bid on behalf of the vendor unless the right to bid is expressly reserved in the particulars or conditions of sale.

2. It is submitted that a similar restriction will be imposed upon a vendor who wishes to bid personally. However, it may be noted that, while section 6 of the 1867 Act makes it lawful for 'the seller or any one person on his behalf' to bid where a right to do so is reserved in the appropriate manner, section 5 merely provides that, where no such right is reserved, the seller may not 'employ any person to bid'. It is thus possible to argue, albeit faintly, that personal bidding is not ruled out.

3. As to the possibility that the Act also requires a clear statement (in whatever form) that a reserve has been fixed, this question remains to be decided in some future case.

(For further reading refer to pages 363 to 369 of John Murdoch's book.)

The Act is interesting because in Sections 5 and 6 the Statute Law relating to the reserve price will be found. The problem is that the sections were poorly drafted and clarification has yet to be defined by the courts. The auctioneer must stipulate the fact that there is a reserve price in the particulars or conditions of sale. Historically this fact had been stated by the auctioneer from the rostrum at the commencement of the sale. However the Act does not state what the position is when the existence of a reserve price is not stated in the particulars or conditions of sale. The lack of case law on these points seems to indicate that the practice of auctioneers covering the matter of the reserve and the right to bid in the conditions of sale and in the particulars has been successful in clarifying the position and preventing confusion leading to litigation.

A grey area is when the right to bid is stipulated but not the fact that the auction is also subject to a reserve. The question, as yet undefined by case law, is whether with the stipulation of the right to bid there is automatically inferred a stipulation that the lot is offered subject to a reserve price. In order to safeguard the position of both the vendor client and the auctioneer, the auction particulars and the conditions of sale must stipulate that the lot is offered subject to a reserve price and that there is also reserved the right to bid. Note that to state that there is reserved the right to fix a reserve is not adequate to safeguard the situation, but rather that the sale is subject to a reserve.

In concluding this chapter on the Reserve Price the missing element is where to pitch the figure. Reference is made to adopting a ten per cent mark down on the market value of the lot. The logic is that by adopting a discount, once the bidding has reached the reserve price and the auctioneer declares that fact at the appropriate moment, then bidding will be stimulated, so raising the actual sale price by competition to market value or above. Remember the earlier comment as to when the bidding on a lot has reached the reserve and the common practice by many auctioneers not to state this fact until the final bid is made and the gavel is about to fall.

However, the fact of life is that, while there are merits in discounting the market value, each lot has to be assessed individually, taking all circumstances into account. Likely bidders, market conditions, the lot itself, and the client all contribute to the eventual decision.

Circumstances arise where the figure may be settled at a greater percentage than ten per cent below the market value, perhaps to clear a portfolio or to dispose of a tertiary commercial holding. Bear in mind that with many instructions, the reserve is agreed with the vendor at the outset of the marketing. Here the percentage may be higher in relation to the market value by the sale date, if values have moved ahead, or lower if they have fallen.

Furthermore, the reserve may be set well above the market value, but careful regard must be paid to the Price Guide because if the reserve is fixed above the Price Guide the auctioneer has misled bidders and will be open to a claim of having given misleading information. Assuming that the Price Guide has been adjusted during the marketing campaign, then in the light of the information on the auction file and especially having regard to offers which have been made or knowledge of a special bidder, the reserve price can be set at a level to take this into account. The risk for the auctioneer when taking this route is that the particular bidder may stop bidding when he senses that the genuine bidding in the room has lapsed and so leave the lot to be withdrawn.

The 'best practice' routine as set by the example of auctioneers over many decades makes the position clear that the existence of the reserve is both printed in the particulars of sale and clearly stated from the rostrum at the commencement of the sale. The Reserve Price is the fundamental lynchpin of the auction process and the success or failure of the actual sale will depend essentially on the level at which it is set.

10 The Auctioneer's Code of Conduct

To the uninitiated man in the street the whole process of an auction, and the authority under which the auctioneer carries out the sale, is shrouded in mystery. The general public views auctions with reservations mainly because historically the workings of the auction process have not been explained and promoted by the landed professions and auctioneers. This situation has changed dramatically over recent years and all the main auctioneers now actively encourage new bidders through the use of explanatory brochures, video films and workshops. For some thinking of attending an auction there remains the fear that if they scratch an ear or even blink, then the auctioneer will take a bid off them! Again there is often a failure to appreciate that the fall of the gavel at, or above, the reserve creates a binding contract. Another frequent misunderstanding is how much they have to pay over on the fall of the gavel – is it 10%, a higher amount or the total sale price?

As previously stated in earlier chapters, the difficulty is that the code of conduct is made up in part from statute law, in part case law, and mainly by the long established practice of the auctioneer over the centuries. Reference has been made to the Royal Institution of Chartered Surveyors and the Incorporated Society of Valuers & Auctioneers 'Guidance Notes for Auctioneers proposing to sell Real Estate at Auction in England and Wales' and here is set out the opinion of the landed professions on 'the best practice' for auctioneers. However, the Guidance Notes are just what the title states – Guidance Notes – and the working auctioneer must be fully conversant with the authority and code of conduct vested in him or her when faced with the scene of the live auction on the sale day. These are essential ingredients to the successful outcome of the auction and other elements are discussed in Chapter 13.

Always at the forefront of his or her mind the auctioneer must retain consistently a mixture of obligations and duties:

- The Duty of Care and best advice to the vendor client
- The Duty of Care to the bidders
- The Duty of Care to the purchaser
- The Duty of Care to the general public
- The Duty of fairness to all participants
- The Duty of openness to all participants

In recent years there has been a steady movement away from *caveat emptor* (let the buyer beware) as we find ourselves faced with a society which requires by legislation more and more consumer protection. When the weight of legislation to underpin consumer protection is added to this trend we find that auctioneers, regarding many facets of the process of selling real property by public auction, are faced with a changing set of rules and constraints which directly affect their conduct. Equally, many auctioneers will say they are one step ahead of this social change and that, by virtue of the process of the auction sale of real property, they have consistently been extremely careful to make certain that, in the interests of their vendor clients, they do not give rise to any circumstances which might invalidate the sale of a lot at auction.

In order to understand the intricacies of this vital element of the role of the auctioneer we will examine each aspect of the elements which combine together to create 'the conduct of the auctioneer'.

As Brian Harvey and Franklin Meisel (1995) Auctions Law and Practice state: 'There are few restrictions placed upon carrying on the business of auctioneer, and no special formal qualifications are required. The only limitations are those arising from the law of contract and certain general statutory provisions relating to companies, partnerships and the like.'

The auctioneer has to have received the authority from the vendor client and this arises usually from his or her formal appointment to act in the sale. Recent statute law in the form of the Estate Agents Act 1979 and the subsequent regulatory regulations require the auctioneer to set out clearly the duties to third parties and the handling of money, particularly deposits. This is in addition to a wide range of requirements relating to the usual agency activities. Those aspects referring to auctions are examined in Chapter 4 and elsewhere in this book.

The authority to act as the auctioneer for a client

The *actual* or *real authority* comes to the auctioneer through the appointment of the firm by the vendor client as set out in the formal written letter. This is referred to in detail in Chapter 2 and it is therefore essential that this letter covers not just the required headings under the Estate Agents Act 1979 and the subsequent regulations, but also the wider issues involved in acting as the auctioneer. In the event of a dispute involving the client or a third party, the court, or the insurers if it is being settled privately between them, will refer in the first instance to that letter of appointment and any subsequent correspondence. The written letter of appointment will therefore expressly give authority to the auctioneer.

While historically the auctioneer relied upon *implied authority* to cover such matters as the signing of the Memorandum of Sale for both the vendor client and the purchaser, regulating the bidding, the right to refuse bids and the right to resolve disputed bids, today the rule is for the auctioneer to cover all these matters in the letter of appointment, thereby leaving nothing to chance or misinterpretation by either the vendor client, or for that matter the courts. If for some reason the client seeks to restrict the authority of the auctioneer, it is important for the auctioneer to make this crystal clear in the particulars of sale and the Conditions of Sale; otherwise, a third party will not be on notice of the fact.

There is a second area of authority which is the *apparent authority*. The apparent authority is the antithesis of actual authority, because the auctioneer in fact has no authority but in law is regarded as being empowered to bind the principal and a third party.

It arises usually when the client has not given any formal instruction to the auctioneer and the auctioneer proceeds as if he had. In reality, it is an unlikely event as the auctioneer will need the formal written authority in order to comply with the provisions of The Estate Agents Act 1979, but it is not unknown for auctioneers to fail to draft the formal written authority sufficiently broadly so as to embrace all aspects of an auction of real property.

Usually, the auctioneer will be instructed to act in the capacity of agent for the vendor client and as such by virtue of the written terms of appointment the authority will be clearly set out. The auctioneer will be acting as agent to the vendor and on the face of it the duty will be no different from that owed when acting in a private treaty sale. However, there are additional duties over and above those required when acting as agent for a sale by private treaty.

In all respects the auctioneer may only act strictly in accordance with the terms of the appointment and that is why the original appointment letter must not only cater for the normal agency matters but also those specific to the auction of real property.

For further information on these legal aspects the reader is referred to Chapter 3: Capacity and Authority and Chapter 9: Sale of Land by Auction in Auctions Law and Practice by Harvey and Meisel (1995). This is an extremely complex and technical area of the law of agency.

The nature of the instructions

It is an essential element of the duty of the auctioneer to achieve a binding contract for the sale of the property on the best terms that can be obtained from the vendor client's point of view.

As described in the previous section, the auctioneer will have the appointment confirmed in writing, setting out his authority. The written instructions must clearly state that the auctioneer has authority not only to sell by auction but also by private treaty, both prior to and after an abortive auction. If the right to sell by private treaty is not stated, then the auctioneer has no such authority and cannot act in this capacity.

There is a grey area here when an auctioneer without the express written authority to sell by private treaty subsequently sells on the contract and memorandum of sale after withdrawing a property either in the room, or later on in their office, at or above the reserve price. Here there might be said to be an implied authority, but to be certain the written instructions must provide for this situation in order to avoid doubt and possible subsequent litigation by a vendor against the auctioneer.

The Conditions of Sale and Memorandum

It is here that the authority of the auctioneer is set out and the Conditions of Sale are where potential bidders and the public at large will find the clauses which govern the role of the auctioneer. The fact of life is that few people, if any, ever read through these clauses, but it is important that not only are auctioneers familiar with them but also that for each lot they are assiduously checked on each and every occasion.

The Conditions of Sale are prepared by the vendor client's solicitors and are usually either the *Standard Conditions of Sale* (Third Edition) as issued by The Solicitors' Law Stationery Society Limited, or closely follow their format. However, some leading auction houses have their own Conditions of Sale and it is essential to examine in detail the auction catalogues in order to identify the variations (see Figure 10.1).

For each sale and, where it is a collective auction, for every lot, there will be Special Conditions relating to the auction which are specific and incorporate a wide range of matters; not only are clauses incorporated in the previous transfer included, but also new clauses which might arise due to a division of the original property or to reflect the instructions of the vendor. The auctioneer will check the Special Conditions especially in order to make certain that they coincide with the particulars and that they are mentioned, if appropriate, in the opening remarks at the auction sale.

In broad terms the various headings covered by the Sale Conditions with particular reference to property auctions include:

1. Name of the firm of auctioneers, but not the actual auctioneer.

2. Name of the seller.

3. Statement that the sale is subject to a reserve price.

4. Statement that the auctioneer or some other person authorised by the seller may bid up to the reserve price.

5. Statement of the auctioneer's right to regulate the bidding.

6. Statement of the auctioneer's right to refuse/decline to accept bids.

7. Statement of the auctioneer's right to resolve any disputes over bids and the fact that the decision of the auctioneer is final. Often this clause will also set

out how the auctioneer will restart the auction if there has been a dispute over with whom the bid lies.

8. Statement that for the avoidance of doubt the contract becomes binding on the fall of the gavel.

9. The requirement of the buyer on the fall of the hammer to sign the memorandum, state his/her name/name of company and address. It is these words which confirm the unique authority for the auctioneer to be able to sign the Memorandum on behalf of not only the vendor, but also the purchaser. The sale is actually contracted on the fall of the gavel.

Memorandum of Sale

Auction Lot Number..............

Address...

Vendor(s)..

I/We..

of..

do hereby acknowledge myself/ourselves to be the Purchaser(s) of the above Lot, described in the within Particulars of Sale for the sum of £................and having paid to Regional Property Services Ltd the sum of £...............as a deposit and in part payment of the purchase money, I/we hereby agree to pay the remainder of the said purchase money and complete the said purchase according to the within Conditions of Sale.

Witness my/our hands this......................One Thousand Nine Hundred and Ninety Eight

Signed...

Full Names of Signatories...........................

Capacity..

<blockquote>

Purchase Price: £..................

Deposit Paid: £..................

Balance Due: £..................

</blockquote>

As Agents for the Vendor we hereby confirm this sale and acknowledge receipt of the above mentioned deposit.

....

On behalf of Clive Emson Auctioneers acting as Agents for the Vendor

Abstract of Title to be sent to................................of.....................................

For the attention of...

Who is/are duly authorised to accept notices on behalf of the buyer(s) for the purposes of this Contract.

Do not detach this page from the Auction Contract Catalogue

Figure 10.1 Example of auctioneer's Memorandum printed in auction particulars
(Courtesy of Clive Emson Auctioneers)

10. In the event of the buyer declining to sign the memorandum the auctioneer has the authority at his/her option to sign on behalf of the buyer, or to re-offer the lot as if it had not been knocked down.

11. The requirement of the buyer to pay a deposit, usually stated as 10% of the purchase price.

12. The rights of the vendor and the auctioneer when the deposit cheque is dishonoured and the consequences that follow.

Misdescription and misrepresentation

This element is in part regulated by statute law, namely the Misrepresentation Act 1967, the Estate Agents Act 1979 and the Property Misdescriptions Act 1991, together with all the subsequent Regulations and Orders following these Acts.

However, property auctioneers have always conducted their sales on the basis that the greatest possible care must be taken over the preparation and production of the particulars. This extends to the Addendum and any remarks made at the rostrum.

Non-disclosure

The auctioneer is under a duty not to mislead. If a statement is made in the particulars or verbally which is inaccurate, then the auctioneer will be at risk of having made a misdescription. This may result in an offence being made under The Property Misdescriptions Act 1991. For example if a building is described as 'substantial' and it transpires that there are structural problems, this may amount to a misdescription. However, if the word 'substantial' was not used and no similar words were used to infer good condition, or absence of structural defects, then it would be reasonable for the auctioneer to rely upon the purchaser to have made their own enquiries.

Puffing

This word relates not to the manner or style by which the auctioneer conducts the bidding but rather the statements which are made at the commencement and during the auction sale. Especially today, with the weight of consumer protection-led legislation, the auctioneer has to be particularly careful as to the validity, accuracy and worth of any statements which are made from the rostrum.

These remarks can be relied on by the bidders and purchaser as being additional to and reinforcing the content of the particulars and any addenda to them.

Fictitious bids, bidding 'off the wall' or 'trotting'

For conducting the bidding there were traditionally two distinctive styles of auctioneer. However, today this is generally no longer the case for reasons which will be explained.

The first style was to take fictitious bids in sequence where there were no genuine bids up to, but not above, the reserve price. This meant that there were any number of fictitious bids, one following the other, and the auctioneer hoped that any genuine bidder would be encouraged to enter into the bidding running up to, or on the reserve. The result would be a successful sale under the gavel.

An opinion which has been expressed, but never tested in the courts, is that this style of bidding by, or on behalf of the vendor, amounts to mis-representation and, assuming that this is true, that it is unlawful conduct on the auctioneer's part giving rise to deception. However, as discussed earlier in this book, with the auctioneer's right to bid and a reserve on the lot, the property cannot be sold until the reserve is reached with a genuine bid at that figure. Furthermore, a vendor will not agree to a sale until an acceptable price is achieved (in these circumstances the reserve), and in any event a vendor has the right to increase the price until the moment when an offer is accepted. The debate appears to centre around the issue of the sequential bidding and whether there is a defence to it. The right of the vendor to refuse bids until an acceptable price is reached and the 'common practice' of auctioneers in a particular locality are reasons put forward. This is an interesting aspect of all types of auctions, both property and chattels, and one which remains to be defined.

The second style is for only one bid to be made on behalf of the vendor and for no further bids to be made until a genuine bid has been made. Then a fresh bid can be made by the auctioneer for the vendor and so on alternately up to, but not above, the reserve price. Once the reserve is reached, then only genuine bids can be accepted. Today, this is the usual method of conducting real property auctions.

Right to withdraw lots and to sell privately before the auction date

The auctioneer should retain the right to withdraw lots and to sell by private treaty, prior to auction. Usually, these reservations are not only stated in the Conditions of Sale, but also in the General Remarks of the particulars and in the advertisements. If these rights are not reserved then the auctioneer on behalf of the vendor client may find a difficult situation arises if, for some reason, it is decided to sell by private treaty or privately or withdraw the lot.

Prospective bidders will spend substantial sums on professional fees and advice prior to attending an auction. Naturally, they will be annoyed if they attend it only to discover at the last moment that the lot in which they are interested is withdrawn or that it has been sold by private treaty beforehand. This situation can be provided for in advance by the inclusion of suitable wording in the auction particulars and on Proxy Bid forms warning potential bidders of the possibilities and asking them to check with the auctioneers as to the current position before attending the sale.

A suitable form of wording in the particulars or catalogue and in the advertising copy along the lines of 'unless previously sold or withdrawn' will put interested parties on notice and protect both the vendor and the auctioneer from the potential situation outlined in the preceding paragraph arising. If a clause to this effect is not included, then there is the possibility that prospective purchasers may have a claim for abortive expenditure incurred in reliance that the property was to be sold by auction on a stated date where it is withdrawn or sold prior.

Right to amalgamate lots

Especially in the case of agricultural properties and residential lots with accommodation land adjoining, the auctioneer will need to retain the right to alter the lotting immediately before the auction in order to maximise the interest with a view to obtaining the optimum sale price. If this right has not been retained, then the auctioneer will not have the necessary authority from the client to alter the lotting from that as printed in the catalogue.

While every care will have been taken when preparing the auction catalogue, it is possible during the marketing that one or more buyers will have been identified who have expressed a desire to bid for specific amalgamations of lots. Depending upon the level of interest and offers the auctioneer will consider carefully the advisability of taking into account this particular interest when determining the lotting.

To take as an example a detached Victorian house set in a reasonably sized garden and separately with good road frontage to one side the old walled vegetable garden, the auctioneer will have marketed the property as two separate lots. However, if the weight of interest and the level of bids is such that all the indications are that a higher figure is likely to be realised under the hammer by selling as one lot, then the auctioneer will amalgamate the two lots as one. In practice, what will actually happen is for the property to be offered as one lot first and if the reserve is not achieved then to offer them separately. This happens rarely these days and it is viewed as poor practice.

The order of sale

Similar comments apply here as with the last section. The auctioneer must retain the authority to vary the order of sale in the light of the interest expressed during the period of marketing. This applies not so much with a major collective sale, but rather where an agricultural estate, a large industrial factory site, or a complicated commercial lot is being sold by auction.

Price Guides

Today the price guide should be a true reflection of the likely realisation price of the lot and, as the marketing progresses, it is desirable that the guide is adjusted to reflect any credible offers which have been received during the marketing of the property leading up to the sale date.

Again, the underlying reasoning here is that the auctioneer must not mislead interested bidders for the lot and so cause them to incur fees unnecessarily. Imagine a derelict farmhouse which on comparative evidence of another recent sale will realise about £45,000. In order to create interest the Press Release and price guide given out states a figure of £35,000. Some potential bidders will be attracted by the apparently low price guide and in the process of preparing to bid for the lot will incur expenditure. Naturally, when they discover that the price guide has increased dramatically, perhaps close to £45,000, they will be frustrated and upset. The auctioneer might give a bracket figure of say £35,000 to £45,000, but a range of this magnitude on such a relatively low realisation figure would be hard to justify where comparative evidence points to the upper limit.

Where price guides are quoted, the auctioneer should include a definition or explanation in the particulars and also warn interested parties that there may be adjustments to the figures in the run-up to the sale day. Usually the particulars contain a statement recommending prospective buyers to keep in touch with the auctioneers on a regular basis. Equally, where they have registered their interest with the auctioneer, all reasonable efforts should be made by the auctioneer to inform them of alterations to the price guide.

Handling of sold lots

When lots are sold while the price is public knowledge the identity of the purchaser is privy to the auctioneer, the vendor client's solicitor and the vendor client. The name of the purchaser must not be disclosed without their specific authority.

Bidding on behalf of potential buyers

The situation will arise where a potential buyer will ask the auctioneer to bid on their behalf because for some reason they will not be present at the auction.

Whatever the circumstances, there is the question of a conflict of interest arising and confidentiality as between the buyer, the auctioneer and the vendor client. The usual practical route is for the auctioneer to anticipate this situation and to discuss with the client as to how to cater for it. The client may have strong views against an apparent divided loyalty as between vendor and bidder. The auctioneer will advise the vendor of the desirability of encouraging the optimum level of interest in the lot and seek to reassure the client that all parties' interests can be safeguarded. This is dealt with by the auctioneer's office appointing another partner or negotiator to represent the bidder and for a 'Chinese wall' to be created so that there can be no transfer of confidential information, especially the level of the likely bid and the reserve price. Absolute trust on both sides is essential.

This situation arises frequently at sales. However, the auctioneer has to be careful to provide for the unexpected, such as last minute alterations to the Special Conditions of Sale, the revelation of some major factor affecting the lot and its likely value, and with telephone bids something going wrong with the telephone connection or in making contact with the bidder.

The acceptance of telephone and proxy bids by the auctioneers usually requires the bidder to have deposited with the auctioneers an amount of the deposit to reflect a sale at the Price Guide.

Most auction catalogues now contain a standard form to be completed by prospective bidders. The form sets out the conditions and terms attaching to the authority and the procedure for handling the deposit and signing the memorandum.

Sale and purchase on behalf of interested parties

The Estate Agents Act 1979 requires the auctioneer to disclose to the vendor and potential bidders any personal interests and the definition here is very wide. Where there are joint auctioneers the requirement also applies.

Handling of unsold lots

Usually, the letter of appointment of the auctioneer will contain an authority for handling the sale of unsold lots at auction. This may also include, as a separate matter, a period of sole agency to run from the auction date for a stated period of 4 weeks or more.

This is important for the auctioneer, as with unsold lots hopefully the auction will have generated interest which can be encouraged to a level where bids are submitted subsequently leading through to a sale. Most auctioneers find that an extremely high percentage of unsold lots at auction are sold within a reasonably short period of time after the sale date.

The wording of the clause needs to make it absolutely clear as to the extent of the authority of the auctioneer in the auction room once the lot has been offered, but remains unsold. With an unsold lot there is the possibility that a sale might be agreed in the room, but the question is whether or not the auctioneer has the authority of the vendor to sign the contract without further reference. When the client is present a decision can be made promptly, but the difficulty arises when the person is absent.

Unless the appointment states to the contrary, the authority may lapse once the auctioneer leaves the rostrum and, in the opinion of many auctioneers, once the sale room is left. To safeguard the situation the auctioneer should provide for the eventuality of unsold lots in the sale room. It is a dangerous assumption that the vendor wishes to sell at or above the reserve once the lot is withdrawn. The auctioneer requires a clear definition as to the circumstances which permits the signing of the memorandum and for how long the authority runs. This is not to be confused with the appointment to act as an agent during the period of sole agency afterwards.

In concluding this chapter it will be seen that the auctioneer has a wide range of duties and responsibilities. These are not only owed to the vendor client but also to prospective bidders and to the general public at large. Over and above any statutory and legal liabilities the auctioneer has an overriding moral obligation to be fair and equitable to all parties involved. The real property auctioneer has everything to gain and nothing to lose by adopting this stance and so will enhance not only his or her personal standing and reputation but also those of the firm and the role of the auctioneer. The real property auctioneer has always held this unique and special position and by virtue of it generates the goodwill and trust of all concerned.

The Code of Conduct, encapsulating the duties and responsibilities of the auctioneer, will be seen as the keystone to the success of the auction and it bodes ill for those who enter the rostrum ill-informed and unaware of its import.

11 Preparations for the Sale Day

The long haul from the initial instruction to offer the property for sale by auction is nearly over, but it is at this stage that the auctioneer must yet again check and double check all the facts and figures, together with every single matter that might in some way or other affect the outcome of the auction. As has been stated many times in the preceding chapters, the auctioneer has to be aware consistently of the need to be fully conversant with everything which has a bearing upon the success or otherwise of the auction. This manifests itself in the duty of the auctioneer to be fair and even handed with all parties to the proceedings, not just the vendor client. Over and above this requirement, there is always the overriding prime duty of care to the vendor client.

Within a few days of the sale date the auctioneer's office follows a standard routine of checking every aspect relating to each lot and this will include the following:

The auction particulars

Read through the original printed particulars, line by line, from start to finish and check against the file for any alterations which might have been made during the marketing of the lot. The auctioneer has to be reassured that either these amendments have been incorporated in the Addendum or they are included in the notes of the announcements which will be made from the rostrum.

Items which need especial care are:

The photograph
Is it accurate and does it fairly represent the lot?

The plan
Is it accurate and does it show the boundaries with ownerships clearly identified?
Does it agree with the legal documents on file?

Leases, tenancies and licences
Are these correctly set out and is the detail accurate?

Easements
Are these correct?

Wayleaves
Are these correct?

Tenure

Is this correctly set out and is reference made to any leases, tenancies, licences and ground leases?

Possession

If vacant possession is to be given of the whole or part, is the date correct?

Completion

Is the date for completion clearly stated?

Sometimes the completion date will not have been stated in black and white in either the Special Conditions of Sale or the Memorandum and so this will have to be agreed with the vendor client and the solicitors.

Also bear in mind that it is not unusual for the completion date to be before the possession date where the land or buildings are let or held over and possession cannot be given to coincide with completion.

The pre-auction sale inspection

Whether it is done by the auctioneer personally, or by a member of the team, it is sensible to re-inspect each lot shortly before the sale. It is amazing how much damage can be inflicted on a substantial building by over zealous would-be buyers and their advisers. Equally, where specific items in the nature of fittings rather than fixtures are stated in the particulars, a check must be made to ensure that these items are still in place.

There are plenty of horror stories, especially with residential lots, and the usual one is along the lines of the vendor removing all the plants and garden ornaments. With an old rectory the story took a different turn when a fine old built-in ash dresser in the kitchen disappeared two days before the auction. The house was empty and obviously whoever had taken the dresser had laboured hard for several hours prizing it out of the walls into which it was built. While it transpired later that it had been stolen by thieves not connected with the rectory in any way, the auctioneer had no alternative but to include an announcement in the preamble to the sale to the effect that the dresser had been stolen and the surrounding masonry damaged. The successful purchaser announced afterwards that their bidding had not been affected as they disliked the dresser and would have removed it anyway!

It is not unusual for the auctioneer to say in the opening preamble to the sale words to the effect that when the lot or lots were inspected several days ago, vandalism was noted together with the removal of some fittings. Therefore, the auctioneers can give no warranty on behalf of the vendors as to the state of repair and condition which may have deteriorated as between the date of inspection by bidders and the sale day. Cases are not unknown where with urban blocks with vacant possession virtually everything that can be stripped out has been physically removed by third parties.

The General and Special Conditions of Sale

Read these through and confirm that any cross-references as between the particulars together with the Addendum and the Special Conditions agree on relevant information such as tenure, possession, and completion. The Special Conditions of Sale may be printed as part of the auction catalogue or be separate and held on the auction file. They will always be made available at the auction.

The Memorandum

Again read the document through and note the basis upon which the deposit is to be held. If the completion date is not mentioned, sometimes through an oversight it is left blank in the Conditions of Sale, check as to whether it is stated here.

The Searches and Enquiries on Contract

Here the Searches and Enquiries on Contract may reveal something which has not come to the notice of the auctioneer. This might be the existence of a footpath or a recently issued Local Authority Order.

The Addendum

Once every single aspect of the particulars has been read through and cross checked against the file, the auctioneer can proceed to prepare the note for the statements which will be made from the rostrum. Alternatively, any alterations will have been checked for their accuracy against the Addendum. For example, with commercial lots a rent review may have been concluded or notices may have been served by either the landlord or tenant.

For collective sales, the usual practice is to prepare an updated Addendum setting out all the amendments which is handed out to all those attending the auction. This ensures that everyone at the auction is aware of the alterations and is fully briefed on each lot before the bidding starts.

While this task may appear at first sight to be time consuming, it is an essential step in the auction procedure where openness, accuracy and fairness to all parties are the keystone of a successful auction sale.

Depending upon the timescale it is preferable for the Addendum to be circulated to all the applicants as soon as it is available. This is considered to be good practice. The information is sometimes also made available on dedicated telephone lines and in the future on the Internet.

The Reserve Price

This subject has been covered in Chapter 9. The file must be checked to confirm that the written authority is on the file. If the reserve is to be discussed and agreed with the vendor client immediately before the sale commences, then make certain that a blank authority is on the file so that this can be completed and signed by the auctioneer and vendor client in the sale room.

If the reserve price is to be agreed immediately before the auction, confirm that the client will come along well before the sale starts.

On occasions the authority for the reserve price will be sealed and the envelope will be opened on the rostrum by the auctioneer immediately before offering the lot. Here, confirm that the authority has been received or that it will be handed in to the auctioneer in the sale room. If it is overlooked and not received, then the lot cannot be offered, to the embarrassment of all concerned!

The sale venue

Quite simply check that the hotel or other venue is expecting you and that there has not been a double booking. Where the venue is a village hall or similar place confirm that the key will be available and where to collect it. Some hotels, particularly if tenanted under long leases, have clauses which preclude sales by auction being held upon the premises. In London and other major cities this point should be checked.

Wherever the sale is held it is essential to check that the appropriate insurance cover is in place, that local authority and fire regulations are complied with, and that the room is of sufficient size.

When selling a run-down Methodist minister's house the vendor had stipulated that the sale was not to be conducted on licensed premises and so the venue was the local village hall in a small hamlet. On the evening of the sale the auctioneer and his clerk arrived in good time only to find both the hall and the adjoining keyholder's cottage in total darkness in spite of a telephone call the day before to confirm the booking. The time was 5.30 pm and the sale was scheduled for 6.30 pm. A degree of panic was evident but just before deciding that the only solution was to break in, a village bus hove into view and duly deposited the keyholder, complete with shopping bags, outside the hall. The clerk's duties are amazingly varied as the evening revealed and the first was to carry the shopping to the cottage and collect the key.

Access was at last gained to the hall, the rostrum set up and everything set out ready for the auction. The public drifted in and settled themselves down, then the lights went out! Thankfully both the auctioneer and clerk were pipesmokers so out with the matches and the game of 'find the fuseboard' commenced with pleas to one and all to remain calm. Once found the full horror of the problem was revealed, it was a slot metered supply and the keyholder had overlooked this fact when confirming the booking! Once again the clerk was dispatched post haste to the inn across the village green to obtain a supply of 50p pieces and by 6.15 pm order was restored to the evening.

No doubt there are many similar tales, especially where electronic systems, multiple telephone links and the like are used. The moral of the story is that one can never check too thoroughly and even then some gremlin will emerge to wrong-foot you!

The solicitors

If they are to be present then a telephone call the day before to remind them is prudent, making certain that they have remembered the time and venue.

The auction case

Once all these steps have been completed the auctioneer will make up his or her auction case. This will contain:

- The auction file

- The legal documents

- The gavel

- The auctioneer's tablet as required by the Auctioneers Act 1845. (On the upper part the auctioneer's name is printed in full, below the address and appended at the bottom the extract of the Auctions (Bidding Agreements) Act, 1927.)

- The extract of the Auctions (Bidding Agreements) Act 1969.

- The auctioneer's copies of the auction particulars or catalogue.

- The Addendum.

- The auctioneer's notes of what is to be said from the rostrum.

The auctioneer's rostrum notes

Once every single aspect of the particulars has been read through and cross-checked against the file the auctioneer can proceed to prepare the notes for the statements which will be made from the rostrum.

The auctioneer needs to set some time aside a day or so before the auction when with a clear head the forthcoming auction can receive his or her undivided attention. After going through the above-mentioned stages and checks the time has arrived to prepare the notes on which the remarks will be made from the rostrum. Every auction sale is a new challenge with its own unique lots and attendant issues and every auctioneer approaches a sale in his or her special style. The end result is that there is no standard format for the notes and the approach for a single lot sale in a country inn will be very different from that for a major collective sale at a London venue.

However, there are some elements which are common to all auctions and no matter how experienced the auctioneer the value of an *aide-mémoire* cannot be underrated. There is always the occasion when something happens to throw your concentration and the list of headings or notes can prove to be the saviour of the hour!

Some auctioneers like to have every word typed out as a script for the auction, while others prefer to have merely a series of longhand headings with the suitable comments alongside. Yet again there are endless variations between these two extremes and at the end of the day it is what works for the particular individual that matters.

Practically speaking, the reason for the notes is to make certain that nothing is omitted and that all the formalities are completed in a flowing and natural manner without lots of embarrassing pauses and hunting through papers and files. The main headings will include:

- The introduction to the auction sale
    The auctioneer's name
    The firm's name

- The property(ies) to be offered
    The order of sale

- Thanking the vendor(s) for their instructions

- Introduce those on the rostrum
    The solicitors
    The clerk

- The auction catalogue

- The Addendum

- Legal matters
    This may be dealt with by the solicitors

- The formalities to be completed by successful bidders

- The Memorandum of Sale

- The Deposit

- Liability for insurance of purchased lots

If there is to be a special charge on successful purchasers for the expedited clearance of cheques, usually a charge of around £12.00, this should be announced when referring to deposits.

Another point to stress to bidders, and one which is frequently overlooked, is that generally on the fall of the gavel the liability for insurance of the lot passes to the purchaser.

For coping with enquiries and questions on lots prior to offering them by auction there are two distinct ways of dealing with this sometimes fraught issue. The older style, still widely adopted for provincial country auctions, is for the auctioneer upon completion of the general introduction to invite questions from the floor. This method will be discussed in detail in Chapter 11: The Auction.

Perhaps as an extension of the London multi-lot auctions, many auctioneers today prefer to state from the rostrum several times, perhaps at ten-minute intervals, the fact that the solicitor(s) is present and anyone with queries should come forward to the rostrum and discuss them, *as no questions will be taken once the auction starts*. Some regard this tactic as a blocking move, but it does have the great benefit from the vendor client's point of view of preventing any 'spoiling' questions by prospective bidders seeking to put off others.

In any event the auctioneer needs to have a reminder in the notes, either to prompt announcements prior to starting the sale on any queries, or at the appropriate slot to invite questions.

The Auction Book

Most auctioneers have a series of auction books. These are a fascinating insight into social history where they cover many years as they record every auction sale, the pattern of bidding, the reserve, the sale price, the name of the buyer, and often a few asides or other wry comments. Sadly, many of these historic records were mislaid or destroyed when auctioneering firms ceased business or were acquired by new owners, but in some cases the records are guarded jealously and continue to be added to on a regular basis today, others have been lodged in local Archive Offices for future reference by researchers.

Each firm will have their own format for the size, style and layout of the book. Preferably it should be a hardback bound book of at least A4 size with numbered pages. In a typical book the lot from the auction catalogue or the relevant part of the particulars will be glued onto the facing left-hand page and at the top of the right-hand page the reserve price will be recorded, occasionally in the auctioneer's code. At the beginning of the auction, after the introductory comments have been completed, the clerk, or occasionally the auctioneer, will open the book and write down the bids as they are made. The use of the book will be enlarged upon in next chapter.

The Clerk

Depending upon the practice of the office, the clerk will usually be responsible for the following:

1. A supply of spare auction particulars

2. A supply of the Addendum

3. The tape recorder and spare tapes

4. Copies of the poster

5. A supply of the firm's promotional material

The clerk will act as an extension of the auctioneer and after the first few sales will adopt a familiar routine, knowing and understanding how the auctioneer approaches the auction and acting as a 'sweeper-up' to make certain that each and every point is covered.

Auction seminars and information packs for buyers

Historically, anyone who wished to attend a property auction for the first time, either took their life in their hands and went along trusting that the gods would protect them, or asked another auctioneer or solicitor familiar with auctions to accompany them as their mentor. Whichever route was adopted for those bidders the auction experience was an awe-inspiring and often frightening experience. Furthermore, it was not unknown for auctioneers to hand the catalogue out and after that refuse to give any further help or advice other than to refer the person to their solicitors.

Today the picture is very different, with many auction houses running excellent Auction Seminars and Teach-ins. These serve a twofold purpose as the auctioneers are able to identify potential bidders and at the same time the bidders can meet the auction team. As part of the process the complete auction procedure from the start of the sale to the signing of the Memorandum and payment of the deposit is explained and demonstrated in detail. Most importantly it will be made clear that the fall of the hammer means that a contractual commitment is made between the final bidder and the vendor.

The pattern for a 'Teach-in' will include:

- A demonstration of the auction
- How do I buy by auction?
- How do I bid at auction?
- Are there risks at buying by auction?

A solicitor, along with the auctioneer and the auction team, will be present and they will not only answer the questions above but also a whole host of queries which have been put to them over the years. The whole emphasis of the gathering is to reassure the bidders and to give them confidence to attend on the sale day.

Another permutation on the seminar is the 'Open Night' or 'Informal Evening' where the auctioneers give a presentation followed by a one-to-one opportunity for bidders to meet the auction team and the vendor client solicitors. This is aimed rather more at talking to the bidders on an individual basis.

Many firms have useful leaflets and information sheets and at least one auction house has a video film on the subject. Many catalogues contain a helpful list of hints and pointers for bidders. However, for those who have not attended a live auction sale there is no substitute for going along to several sales to sense the atmosphere of the room and the way that the auctioneer conducts the sale.

The steps that a bidder should take before attending an auction are:

1. Obtain a copy of the auction particulars.
2. If not stated in the particulars, ask the auctioneer for a price guide.
3. Inspect the property.
4. Ask the auctioneer if there is a 'Buyer's Information Pack', as this may include a report on condition, contract, searches and other information.
5. Consult solicitors.
6. Arrange for a survey or specialist report.
7. Confirm that the necessary finances are in place including funds on the sale day to pay the deposit.
8. Discuss the upper limit to bid at auction with the surveyor after taking into account the result of the survey, comments from the solicitors and availability of funds.

9. Check with the auctioneer as to how the deposit can be paid, i.e. personal cheque, banker's draft, cash or the like.
10. A few days prior to the sale, check with the auctioneer to see if there have been any amendments.
11. On the sale day arrive in good time and listen carefully to all the announcements.
12. Bid clearly and positively.

The whole approach by auction houses today is to dispel the myth that auctions are strictly for the experienced person. Many innovations have been made to attract new bidders into the auction room and the overall effect has been to increase substantially the numbers attending sales or leaving proxy bids. This is to the benefit of all parties participating in the sale and auctioneers are actively seeking new ways and approaches to achieve a smooth path to a binding contract between buyers and sellers.

12 Bidding for Buyers

In Chapter 10 the relationship between the auctioneer, the vendor client and prospective bidders when asked to bid on their behalf at auction was discussed in terms of internal office systems and procedures. Another scenario arises when an agent is asked to bid for a lot at auction. For most auctioneers, this form of instruction is both a challenge and a pleasure, with the reward being the successful purchase of the lot in the face of keen competition in the room. However, life is not that simple and before rushing off to the sale the agent must take careful steps to regulate the position both with the client and with the auctioneer who will be conducting the auction.

Appointment of an agent to bid

On the basis that the client has completed all the necessary enquiries, that the appropriate professional advice has been obtained and that the financial arrangements are in place the client will be instructing the agent to bid up to a specific figure. The first step that the agent must take is to obtain a written instruction from the client to bid on their behalf (see sample form at end of chapter).

The difficulty with any form of proxy bidding authority is how to cope when the rules are changed by the introduction of the unexpected. Perhaps only part of the property is with possession, or the Local Authority has placed an Order on the building, and the auctioneer announces the fact from the rostrum. Without question, the purchase of a property is too great an undertaking for anything as fundamental as a last minute change of a key factor affecting value and use to be left in the lap of the gods. The last minute changes which can be disclosed from the rostrum are endless and the agent cannot cover every eventuality.

For the agent and the prospective bidder the most likely problem is communication, even in these days of sophisticated telephone systems. While the bidder may be prepared to give the agent discretion to act as he or she feels appropriate, it is a dangerous move on the part of the agent. What is unimportant or irrelevant to the agent may well be of sufficient concern for the client to withdraw from the auction.

Practically speaking, the agent must discuss at length with the client the problems which could arise over such issues, actual and anticipated. Where the client is well known to the agent and this type of instruction is regularly undertaken the agent may feel sufficiently confident to accept a degree of flexibility here, but this will inevitably result in an uncomfortable grey area with the risk lying with the agent. In the event of a subsequent falling out over a purchase when an alteration has been made by the auctioneer at the last minute without reference by the agent to the client, there is the interesting question as to how the agent's insurers will view the situation so far as Professional Indemnity Insurance is concerned.

Usually, in order to protect both the agent and the client from any mis-understanding the preferred appointment will state that the agent will not bid for the property in the event of a last minute change. This may be made subject to a proviso that the agent will use his or her best endeavours to contact the client.

Appointment of the auction house to bid

Many of the major auction houses that regularly conduct collective sales offer a service to bidders who are unable to attend the sale to bid on their behalf. The Proxy Form is printed in the catalogue and the bidder can complete the Proxy Form and post or hand it in together with a cheque or banker's draft to cover the deposit to the auctioneers (see sample form at end of chapter).

The wording on the Proxy Form will include something to the effect of '...and have knowledge of any announcements to be made from the rostrum of any amendments relating to the relevant Lot. Announcements can and should be checked by bidders on the day of the auction between 9 am and one hour before the commencement of the auction.' This arrangement places the responsibility of disclosure fairly and squarely on the bidder. Whatever the arrangement reached between the auctioneer and the bidder, there must be a clear understanding in the interests of both parties on this issue of late disclosure and for it to be recorded in writing to avoid any area of doubt.

Relationship between the agent and the auctioneer

Another area which can easily be overlooked by an agent when asked to bid at an auction, especially as such an instruction often comes in at the last moment, is the relation between the agent, his or her client, the auctioneer and the vendor of the property. Simply put, if the agent is the successful bidder who is the purchaser, the agent or his client? To safeguard the agent's position the agent must before the auction commences notify the auctioneer that he is acting for a third party and that in the event of success the auctioneer will accept the signature on the Memorandum by the agent with the added wording 'as agent for XYZ'. There is no need to disclose the name of the client when disclosing the fact to the auctioneer before the sale starts, so confidentiality can be maintained, but if the bid is successful the name and address will be entered on the Memorandum of Sale.

Bidding at the auction for the client

Every agent will have their own approach to bidding at auction, but there would seem to be little point in starting the bidding and then relentlessly plugging away against the auctioneer or other bidders until either the lot is secured or the authority exhausted. Some will wait for a lull in the bidding before starting, others will hold back until the auctioneer indicates that the bidding is at or above the reserve and others wait until the final bid is made and the auctioneer is about to bring down the gavel. Yet another variation is for the bidder to make a substantial and bold opening bid in the hope that this level and manner of bid will 'psych' out anyone else! It can work.

There are practical reasons for holding back until the reserve is reached when acting for a bidder. If there are no bids, or the bidders dry up before the reserve is reached, there is the very real opportunity of purchasing the lot by private treaty immediately after the sale in the auction room at the reserve price or even a lower figure if the vendor is present. There is a problem with this approach because not all auctioneers make it clear where the reserve lies and, if the figure is not reached, the first indication may be when the lot is withdrawn. This is where knowledge of the auctioneer and his or her approach to conducting the sale are of advantage. There is also the strong possibility that the vendor has agreed to a low reserve price in the room, but when offering the withdrawn lot by private treaty afterwards will seek a markedly higher figure.

As an aside, a West country auctioneer went to bid on behalf of a retained farmer for a block of accommodation land at a local auction. To say the very least the particulars were brief and contained no reference to a reserve price, or to the conditions of sale under which the lot was to be offered. As the client owned the adjoining land and knew the history of the lot he had not consulted his solicitor, but he had made enquiries of the Local Authorities. At the appointed hour the auctioneer called for quiet in the bar and much to the surprise of our auctioneer merely made a brief reference to the lot and then straight away invited bids. Someone in a smart suit along the bar opened the bidding at a figure well below the value and after a short run against the auctioneer stopped bidding. There followed a long pause while the auctioneer sought to bring a new face into the bidding and then made a bid patently on behalf of the vendor. At this point our auctioneer made a bid, still well below the value to the tune of some 15%, although there had been no comment that the reserve had been reached or was close by. One more bid followed from the auctioneer on the rostrum and then another long silence after which the auctioneer announced that he had no alternative in the light of no further active bidding but to withdraw the lot. The time had now arrived for our auctioneer to walk forward to the rostrum and to point out to the auctioneer and the solicitor that at no time during the auction proceedings had any reference been made to the reserve or to the Conditions of Sale. Furthermore, no reference was made to them in the auction particulars and so both the farmer and our auctioneer considered that the auction had been conducted without the safety net to the vendor of a reserve. In consequence, after some heated exchanges and to the great embarrassment of all concerned the Memorandum was completed in the name of the farmer at the last bid which our auctioneer had made, some 15% below the market value. Apart from the obvious lessons here, the main point is that when an agent is instructed to attend an auction to bid on behalf of a client it is essential that the agent is familiar with auction procedures and law in the pursuit of achieving the purchase at the best price for his client.

Relationship between vendor and auctioneer where bids are on the book

On the face of it, the auctioneer is in a very invidious position when an authority to bid on behalf of a bidder is accepted, as that person, by virtue of having given the authority, has disclosed that they are keen to purchase and most importantly, the level of their bid. It is not an uncommon situation for the auctioneers to receive a number of authorities to bid and, thus on the face of it, they have a clear picture of the level of interest and value of the bids for the lot in question. In fact, with the auction of real estate this is not the case as will be explained.

Now this is an interesting situation, as it challenges the basic tenet that an auctioneer cannot serve two masters at the same time. In order to overcome the likelihood of a damaging conflict of interest between the seller and likely buyers, as a first step the auctioneers will discuss the problem with the vendor client. The consent of the client must be obtained to accept instructions to bid from prospective buyers and also that the existence of, and the amount of, the bid will not be revealed to him, as confidentiality must be maintained on all sides.

Often it is difficult for vendor clients to grasp the fact that knowledge which is available within one firm of auctioneers who are acting for him on the sale cannot be made available to him. However, when it is shown that by actively helping prospective bidders to participate in the auction increases the competition in the room, hopefully the client will agree to the firm acting for proxy bidders.

Auctioneers have long risen to the challenge of seeking ways by which interest in lots can be increased in the room and, in parallel, the way in which confidentiality can be protected. The auctioneers have to protect their integrity and to ensure that their duty of care and best advice is not undermined.

The solution for the auctioneer is twofold. First a system has to be put in place to create an impenetrable barrier so that confidential information is contained strictly within clearly defined boxes within the office. The auction file for the vendor client must not be open to prospective bidders and vice versa. This may be achieved by setting up entirely separate departments to deal with the two distinct activities. More commonly the partner dealing with the client will also be in touch with the proxy bidders. That partner will make absolutely clear to both parties the existence of the other party, but under no circumstances the level of the proxy bids. Often this is referred to as erecting 'Chinese walls', and the effect is for no information on proxy bids to be disclosed to vendors.

Remember that this activity relates to instructions to bid and not offers received during the marketing period running up to the sale date. Quite simply, the former is privileged information between the bidder and the auctioneer's office and the second is not as it has been disclosed to the vendor client. This leads to the setting of the reserve price and it will be seen that only the latter is available to the auctioneer when advising on this matter. If a prospective bidder thought for one moment that their bid was going to be disclosed to the vendor and used for fixing the reserve price against him this would immediately destroy the integrity of the auction house.

The second step is for the auctioneer to make it crystal clear to the bidder that while an authority or proxy bid can be accepted, under no circumstances can any advice be given, including value, in relation to the lot. The bidder must make their own enquiries and take their counsel from separate professional advisers. All that the auctioneer can do is to implement their instruction on the proxy bid at the sale.

By separating these roles within the office the auctioneer can and frequently with collective auctions does succeed very successfully in maintaining absolute integrity towards both the vendor client and bidders, and at the end of the day achieve consistently satisfactory results in the sale room.

Some firms simplify the handling of proxy bids by directing that they are submitted in sealed envelopes, clearly marked that they are a proxy bid. These are taken to the sale room and opened by the auctioneer or the clerk after the reserves have been fixed and immediately before the commencement of the sale proceedings.

Implementing proxy bids

If proxy bids are submitted in sealed envelopes, they are opened in the sale room by someone other than the auctioneer and, once the reserves have been fixed, entries are made on the auction book or a member of staff is delegated to bid.

In the case of telephone bidding, again members of staff are allotted bidders and as the time draws near to offer the lot, a telephone call is made and contact made. The bidding and any other comments are relayed over the line by the member of staff who, in turn, carries out the instructions of the bidder. Generally, the instruction with respect to the upper figure is limited to the maximum bid as represented by the deposit sent in with the Telephone Bid form (see sample form at end of chapter). This is 10% of the maximum price that the person intends to bid.

At important sales it is not uncommon for there to be several telephone bidders as well as proxy bids on the auction book.

Typical Proxy Bid Authorisation form where an Agent is to bid on behalf of a person

The undersigned hereby authorises.....(agent's name)............
of Messrs ....to bid as his agent for
...........................(address of property).......................
....

referred to as Lot Number...........as described in the attached auction particulars which is to be offered for sale by public auction on
......(date)...... at....(venue)...... by Messrs ....(auctioneer's name).............

In the event of any alterations or amendments to the auction particulars, the General and Special Conditions of Sale or any other matters and information relating to this lot which have not been previously disclosed this authority is revoked forthwith.

The bid shall not exceed £...................(in figures) and as my agent you are authorised to sign the Memorandum of Sale stating that you are acting as my agent, disclosing to the auctioneer my name and address, and paying the deposit.

I, the undersigned, attach my/our cheque drawn in accordance with the General and Special Conditions of Sale in the sum marked 'not exceed' £...............(in figures)

Signed...Client.   Dated......................
Address..
....
Name and Address of Solicitors............................
....

Note: a copy of the auction particulars is to be attached.

Telephone Proxy Bidding form. Note caveats on telephone connections and auctioneer's announcements.

If you wish to bid by telephone in relation to a property being offered in this auction, please complete this form.

The Telephone Bid Form should be sent to us by Recorded Delivery to reach us the day prior to the Auction. We accept no responsibility for any Telephone Bid Forms that are mislaid, lost or improperly completed.

We will endeavour to telephone you on the day of the auction, a couple of Lots prior to the actual Lot being offered. It is essential that you are available.

Your solicitor should be supplied with a copy of this form.

Auction Date...............................Lot No..........
Property..

I hereby irrevocably authorise ....to complete an Auction Contract on my behalf for the purchase of the above property up to the highest bid made by me. I enclose a banker's draft, building society cheque or solicitor's client account cheque equal to 10% of the maximum purchase price that I intend to bid (minimum £100). Cheques to be made payable to ....

I have read and understand the Telephone Bidding Guidelines. I do not and will not hold you liable for being unable to reach me by telephone, or for any interruption with the telephone system during the auction. I have obtained legal advice in connection with this Form and the Auction Contract. I also accept that it is my responsibility to check for any amendments which may be read out by the auctioneer prior to the commencement of the auction.

Signed..

Purchaser's full name..
Purchaser's address...
....
Telephone number & Extension......................................
Solicitor's Name...
Solicitor's Address...
....
Solicitor's Telephone number..........................Fax.............

Proxy Bid Authorisation to the Auctioneers

Date of Auction....................Lot Number...............

I hereby instruct and authorise you to bid on my behalf in accordance with the terms and conditions attached hereto and I understand that should my bid be successful the offer will be binding upon me. I authorise you to record such bidding and instructions in order to avoid any doubts or disputes.

Address of Lot...
Maximum Bid Price £.............Words........................
Cheque for 10% Deposit.............................enclosed

Purchasers Details
Full Name...
Company............................. Position.............
Address...
TelephoneBusiness............. Home.................

Solicitors...
    Telephone...................... Fax.................

Signature of Prospective Purchaser........................
Date....................

Important - Do not detach from the Auction Particulars. Return completed with your cheque for the deposit

13 The Auction

After many weeks of preparation the actual day of the auction sale has arrived. For the auctioneer and the team it is not just a case of turning up at the sale venue and taking the sale, but rather there must be a period of careful preparation beforehand to ensure that the very best results are achieved. For the auctioneer with an early evening sale, to work through a busy agency day from the office and then at 5.30 pm to scoop up the file and dash 12 miles to the venue, arriving on the late side and then with an obviously cursory attitude to conduct the auction, is both patently failing in the duty of care to the vendor client and delivering a hammer blow to the goodwill of the firm of auctioneers, let alone demeaning the worth of auction and the standing of the profession.

Some years ago in a Cotswold market town an auction of a delightful cottage needing some renovation work was advertised by a well-established firm of local auctioneers. The venue was the main hotel in the town and the time set for 6.30 pm. About 5.45 pm people began to drift in and with the bar open at 6.00 pm there was soon a goodly crowd in the large public bar where the auction was to be conducted. However, without the reassurance of the landlord everyone could have been forgiven for questioning whether or not they had come on the correct evening. Nowhere was to be seen any reference to the auction so shortly to occur, no posters, no auctioneer or staff, absolutely nothing!

By 6.25 pm even the landlord was becoming worried and the noise level in the bar was rising sharply, but the general atmosphere was humorous. Still nobody had appeared on the scene from the auctioneers and just as some were beginning to think of calling it a day and going home, the bar door flew open and in charged the auctioneer. To say that he was muttering darkly under his breath was an under-statement. Obviously, the last afternoon appointment had overrun and then back at the office a series of telephone calls had delayed him even further. His demeanour and attitude was veering towards the antagonistic and heightened by a comment that there were too many people in the bar! The sale eventually began at 6.45 pm with no apology from the auctioneer for the late start and the generally shambolic proceedings which followed. It was so bad that some of those present even walked out.

The purpose of this anecdote is to underline the vital need for the auctioneer and the team to ensure that all the hard work that has gone into preparing the auction and marketing is not thrown away by lack of attention and insufficient preparation for the sale itself. This is the ultimate test of the auction process and the ability of the auctioneer. The judge – the vendor client – and the jury – those present – will determine the verdict of the success or failure of the auction, not merely on the sale result, but also from the manner in which the auctioneer has conducted the whole proceedings of the auction.

The auctioneer

Preparation for the sale day falls into two distinct parts for the auctioneer and the team. The first part has already been covered in the last chapter, namely the checking and assembly of the facts and documentation. The second is less obvious but of equal importance. This is for the auctioneer to achieve the correct state of mind and attitude to handle the auction proceedings. Every auctioneer has their own way of achieving this state of mind and many will admit freely that they would rather be 1,000 miles away and to having to cope with a considerable degree of nervousness. This is not unusual and it is all part of the process of achieving a high state of awareness. It is not dissimilar to the actor or singer before the curtain is raised for a first night. Indeed seasoned auctioneers say that, if you do not go through this phase before an auction, then you are likely either to be too self-confident or too laissez-faire and so liable to make mistakes.

An auction sale is a blend of theatre and a highly complex exercise involving the sale of property, with many of the participants nervous in the extreme. The auctioneer has to retain a calm and authoritative attitude throughout the sale, being fair and even handed with all concerned. This is often a taxing task and akin to walking a tightrope!

A few simple and obvious thoughts for the auctioneer are:

1. Allow sufficient time for preparation. When preparing ensure that you are isolated from external interruptions, such as telephone calls and staff. You need to concentrate on the task in hand without distractions, no matter how well meant!

2. Read through and check your notes for the comments and statements which you will be making from the rostrum.

   Bear in mind that what you have to say may influence bidders and their attitudes to particular lots. Make certain that your remarks are in a logical and clear order with no room for confusion. Clarity is essential.

3. Check that you have all the necessary files and papers.

4. Check that you have your auctioneer's tablet and the extracts of the Auctions (Bidding Agreements) Act for display.

5. Check that you have your gavel.

6. Check the tape recorder and tapes.

7. Last, but not least, check your appearance. Always be neatly turned out and well presented. Remember that all eyes will be upon you at the centre of the stage on the rostrum!

The auction case

Usually for provincial auctions the auctioneer will collect up everything required for the sale into an auction case and glued on the inside of it will be a check list to act as a further reminder. An old medium-sized suitcase fulfils this task adequately.

The auction clerk

Another important role player in the auction is the clerk. To outsiders the role that this person plays is not appreciated, but it is essential to the smooth running of the sale and its successful outcome. The clerk should be regarded as an extension of the persona of the auctioneer and so ideally is someone who is not only familiar with the lots but also experienced in the role of a clerk..

Quite often the clerk will double up as the relief auctioneer and the traditional route for the trainee auctioneer is to act as the auctioneer's understudy, so gaining first-hand knowledge of the intricacies of the auction process. Every auctioneer has their own variation on the style and approach to the auction and the team handling the sale. Much will depend on the type of sale, whether it is a collective sale or an individual lot, and the venue. Also, circumstances will be different as between an auction held in a major London or regional city hotel and a country inn.

The clerk will be responsible for checking out the sale venue and setting up the sale room on the day. This includes making certain that:

1. There is a sale board outside the venue entrance.

2. The way to the actual sale room is clearly signed.

3. The refreshment facilities are up and running.

4. The seating is laid out correctly, usually in theatre style.

5. Auction particulars and the Addendum are displayed on side tables in adequate quantities for anyone requesting copies.

6. The rostrum and top table are laid out correctly.

7. Adequate side tables are provided for vendor clients' solicitors.

8. The statutory auction tablets are displayed clearly visible to those present.

9. Any electronic systems are operating correctly. This includes the recording of the auction proceedings, whether by an audio or video system.

10. In-house promotion material is displayed along with details of future sales.

Thinking of the role of the clerk, there was a prominent auctioneer who sold regularly in the ballroom of a main county hotel. Upon pain of death, the clerk in addition to his normal duties, always had to include a number of large double sheets, all cleanly laundered, in the auction suitcase. At the behest of the auctioneer these sheets had to be fixed over all the tall wall mirrors behind and to the side of the rostrum in order to obscure the reflection of the room from those present. He claimed that an observant person would be able to spot in the mirrors where the bids lay and so assess the strength of the opposition!

Ideally, if the auctioneer has not been handling the sale personally the clerk will be familiar with the lots, the vendors and those interested. This means that he or she will easily be able to identify the likely bidders and point out them and their position in the room to the auctioneer before the sale starts. Another benefit is that for nervous bidders there is a familiar face on the rostrum in addition to the auctioneer which helps to reassure them.

Once the auction starts the clerk may have to write down the bids and their identity. This is not always the case and the method and practice of recording the bids varies widely. In any event the clerk will have to keep a weather eye open for any intending bidders who in the heat of the moment the auctioneer might have missed, something which can happen even with the most experienced auctioneers.

Spotters or runners

With major collective sales it is sensible to have several employees of the auctioneers positioned around the sale room. Their duty is to identify the successful bidders of the various lots and, depending upon the system for the payment of deposits and signing the Memorandums of Sale, either to obtain their name and address or to take them up to the side tables where the legal formalities are being completed as the auction progresses.

If the reader has the opportunity to attend an auction in USA an interesting extension of this role may be seen in action. Here the spotter stands alongside a bidder as soon as that person starts to bid, and from then on encourages them with plenty of gestures and remarks to make certain that, not only the auctioneer, but also the whole room knows that they are bidding! Some may consider that all this showmanship is rather going overboard, and indeed that there may be deemed to be an element of coercion. However, some first time buyers at auction find comfort and reassurance from having a member of the auctioneer's staff beside them when bidding.

The auction sale

The appointed hour for the sale has arrived and now the auctioneer, the vendor clients and bidders are to experience the true test of the market. The auctioneer has a special and unique role to play here and must be able to gauge the gravitas of the day and to measure the mood of the company in the room, adjusting his own stance and approach to the feedback. Whatever happens, the auctioneer must take care not to be fazed or thrown off line by the unexpected. This can range from a waitress dropping a tray of glasses during the carefully prepared opening remarks to someone who has the sole objective of putting other bidders off a lot by asking awkward questions and generally being difficult. A golden rule is never under any circumstances to be rude or offensive to a member of the public, and certainly never to lose your temper; always remain composed, polite and in command of the whole proceedings.

Auction is in part pure theatre and it is not uncommon actually to be able to sense this feeling of tension and anticipation in the air at the outset of the sale. A seasoned auctioneer will 'read' the feeling of the company and react accordingly, either adding to the sense of theatre or calming down those present.

By way of starting the auction proceedings the auctioneer will welcome everyone and then introduce him or herself and the firm they represent, also making reference to any joint auctioneers and introducing anyone present on the rostrum from them. Next, anyone else on the rostrum will be introduced, especially the clerk and any solicitors acting for the vendors who are present. The detail here will depend upon the type of sale and how many lots are being offered. The importance of the auctioneer's notes can be understood more clearly now, for faced with some 5 to 10 minutes of introductory speech, it is all too easy to miss a vital section. As a double check each point as it is covered must be ticked off and the clerk following the speech on a copy of the notes also will mark off each section as it is completed.

Part of the act in coping with the lead into the actual commencement of the bidding is to cover all the various sections and areas which need to be highlighted clearly, smoothly and in the minimum of time. In the main, those present will be well prepared and there should be nothing new to add to their fund of knowledge. However, it cannot be stressed too strongly that the auctioneer is under a duty to spell out clearly what is being offered and his powers, duties and obligations to all present. As stated previously, the auctioneer will now be demonstrating not only his or her skill on the rostrum but also the essential ingredient of fairness and an even hand to everyone bidding for a lot, as well as to the vendor clients.

Questions from the floor

Once the introductory remarks are completed the auctioneer may pause and invite questions on any aspect of the lots about to be offered for competition. This is not the common practice in major collective sales and, indeed, increasingly with provincial auctions. Some would say that this practice of excluding questions detracts from the atmosphere and adversarial nature of an auction. To exclude questions at this stage the clerk or auctioneer will announce to the room at regular intervals, say every 10 minutes, in the period before the sale starts that the solicitors are present and anyone with outstanding queries must come up to the rostrum to discuss them. Furthermore, there will be no opportunity to raise questions from the floor once the sale proceedings are commenced. Auctioneers will cover this position further by stating in the auction particulars that prospective bidders '...will be deemed to have read and considered the Particulars, Conditions and Addendum and have full knowledge of these and all documents and other matters referred to whether they have inspected them or not. Furthermore they will not be read out in the room and questions on any matters will not be allowed.'

The interesting question is, what happens if someone persists in trying to raise a question from the floor of the room? Experience over many years on the rostrum has shown that overall questions are raised, not so much to inform and add to the pool of knowledge about a particular lot, but rather to try to dampen competitive bidding. This is done by introducing through the question an area of doubt, uncertainty, or a new fact which appears to downvalue the lot. The question might be along these lines: 'Mr Auctioneer, are you aware that my surveyor has identified the mushrooms in the back store room as not being mushrooms but dry rot fungus spores and that the infestation spreads right up the two floors above to the roof?' Now while everyone present has doubtless taken their own advice on the interpretation of the dry rot, they will perhaps not have seen it as such a major problem with the inferred view by the questioner that the roof is also affected. This line of questions to the auctioneer is known as 'damping'.

Going back to the issue at the beginning of the previous paragraph, given that the necessary steps had been taken prior to the beginning of the sale, then the auctioneer would merely restate the position over questions and decline to allow it to be asked. The standard reply would follow from the auctioneer if the questioner persisted with trying to put the point, with 'In that case you had better not bid for the lot.'

Where questions are taken, the auctioneer will be well advised to brief the solicitor representing the vendor and to agree on how and who will respond initially to any questions. Whoever replies should bear in mind that the reply has the strength of any statement in the particulars or Addendum and so the simple rule is to think carefully before responding. Replies must be factual, and expressed to avoid being led into a discussion. Always keep a measured tone; never show annoyance or lose your temper.

All comments and statements made at this stage become part of the contract. Indeed a statement in the form of a 'caveat' by the auctioneer or solicitor cannot negate the import of legislation. The auctioneer must avoid in the heat of the moment making any flippant or misleading remarks.

Some years ago a large block of single bank salmon fishing on the River Wye was offered at Hereford. The title to the fishing had its origins in estate records going back to the seventeenth century. With various sales off and changes in ownership over the years there were a number of interesting aspects relating to the title which in part relied on possession and use together with statutory declarations for some rods. After the introduction the auctioneer invited questions and from the rear of the ballroom came the inevitable question challenging the root of title to several lengths of the fishing. The auctioneer replied immediately saying. 'Sir, you have had adequate opportunity to make your enquiries about this issue and if you are still in doubt I can but advise you not to bid.' Then he went on to start the bidding for the first lot and was obviously labouring hard to achieve a reasonable pace of bidding and was still well below the reserve. The man who had put the question on the title made a bid and rather than move the bidding on, the auctioneer put up his hand and pointing to the fellow said: 'Ladies and gentlemen, you will be pleased to note that apparently the gentleman at the back of this ballroom is happy with the title as he has just made the last bid, your bid, Sir.' Upon which the bidding erupted and there followed an extremely successful record breaking sale. Here we see the auctioneer thinking on his feet, unscripted and turning an uncomfortable situation into a strong selling point.

The bidding

Unlike local furniture and contents sales where most of the lots are offered without reserves and there are always dealers present who will start the bidding, albeit at low prices, real property auctions are quite the opposite. Usually bidders will be extremely reticent in starting the bidding and the auctioneer will have to use all his skills in trying to draw out the first bid, known as the maiden bid. For every lot the auctioneer will have in the back of his mind the level of the maiden bid, tempered against the reserve.

On those rare occasions where there is a sealed reserve, the auctioneer has a golden opportunity to inject a sense of drama when the envelope is handed across and is opened. Suitable words might be along the lines of: 'Well, ladies and gentlemen I see that I am instructed to offer this lot at an extremely favourable reserve, bid up, this is your chance!'. As said this is unusual, and commonly the auctioneer will be faced with either opening the bidding or seeking out a bidder in the room.

To start the bidding the auctioneer may invite bids, then following deathly silence begin to float out a figure. The approach here varies widely, ranging from starting with suggesting a figure slightly above the reserve and then promptly dropping down in steps to the price at which it is hoped to start. Danger areas for the auctioneer are when a maiden bid (the first bid) is made above or on the reserve as it may prove difficult or impossible to achieve any further bids. Remember that the auctioneer cannot bid above the reserve price unless there is a specific clause to this effect in the Conditions of Sale. This is very unusual and the RICS Guidance Notes state under Section 2.1.2 (vii) 'It is strongly recommended that the Auctioneer does not accept instructions where the vendor requirees the right to bid the reserve or over the reserve.' Assuming that this is the case with no further bids, then the maiden bidder will have successfully purchased the lot!

Alternatively, and generally with collective sales, the auctioneer will try to open the bidding on the lower limit of the Price Guide or slightly above, and then, given active bidders, the reserve will be quickly achieved leading to the final and successful bid, generally within a relatively short timespan of a few minutes.

The pattern of the bidding might be as follows with a Price Guide of £37,000 to £40,000 and a reserve set at £39,000:

Auctioneer £37,000

Bidder £38,000

Auctioneer £38,500

Bidder £39,000 on the reserve

Now, if there is a lull in the bidding the auctioneer can announce that the property will be sold, or is in the room, or some similar expression to convey clearly to everyone that the lot will be sold to this bidder, or if there are further bids to the highest and final bidder. Again auctioneers have individual styles on how they handle this situation, and by attending auctions the reader will quickly grasp how this is dealt with on each occasion.

Every auctioneer has his or her own personal method for conducting and controlling the bidding, the increments and stating whether or not the reserve has been reached or passed. The permutations of the bidding patterns are endless and this is why auctioneers must be constantly thinking on their feet. The first challenge is to start active bidding, the next is to reach the reserve on the correct increment so that a genuine buyer bids at that figure, and the final challenge is to obtain that last final bid on which the gavel falls. As stated previously, there is no substitute for attending as many auctions as possible to study each auctioneer in action and to watch carefully as each lot is offered.

How people bid and identifying them

It would be nice to say that everyone bids in a similar style and manner but life is not that simple and, depending upon the type of sale, the auctioneer is likely to be faced with a wide range of bidders from the experienced self-assured dealer to the extremely nervous first-time buyer. As the auctioneer will be anxious to maintain a smooth- flowing pattern of the proceedings, it is essential both to pick up a new bidder and at the same time to make it absolutely clear exactly whose bid has been accepted.

The auctioneer might work along these lines:

I am bid £28,000.
The bid is yours, sir, front row centre.
Now I am looking for an increase of £2000.

                                                                                        £30,000.
Thank you. On the pillar at the back of the room left side.

                                                                                        £32,000.
At the front.

                                                                                        £34,000.
A fresh bidder, centre right with the red tie.

                                                                                        £35,000.
I will accept a £1000 increase.
On the pillar.

                                                                                        £36,000
At the front.

                                                                                        £37,000
On the pillar.

                                                                                        £38,000
Centre.

A pause in the bidding. In addition to general comment to give bidders a chance to decide whether to go on, the auctioneer will say the bidding is in the centre right and against you in the front row and against you at the back.

The auctioneer will also make great use of his or her hand pointing and by the level and inference of the voice hopefully imparting the tempo and speed of the rate of bidding. This is where the ability of the auctioneer to control those present comes into play and the manner by which this is exercised goes a long way towards creating the theatre of the occasion.

Obviously, the approach to the actual sale will depend on the number of lots being offered and there will be a very different attitude by the auctioneer faced with 100 lots at a major collective sale as compared with a provincial two lot sale in the country inn. For the major sale the proceedings are bound to be more formal and clinical as there are a large number of lots to be offered and the auctioneer has little time to dwell between bids. The rate of selling at a major collective sale is about 3 minutes for each lot, as compared with a country single lot sale where the auction from start to finish ranges from 15 to 30 minutes.

The bidder must ensure that the auctioneer or the clerk is aware that they are bidding. Some auction houses have now adopted a system of registration for major sales on a similar basis to the Fine Art auctioneers. This involves all prospective bidders being issued with an unique number and sometimes a paddle or card to match. To bid the person then either raises the paddle or, if these are not issued, bids in the traditional manner. The use of this system means that all those who wish to bid register with the auctioneer before the sale starts. However, the majority still rely on the bidder making a positive gesture such as waving the catalogue, a hand, or making some other positive movement to catch the eye of the auctioneer or the clerk.

The benefit of the registration of prospective bidders from the auctioneer's viewpoint is that they have advanced knowledge of the level of interest and how many of the enquiries and viewings have resulted in genuine interest.

One of the danger areas from the auctioneer's point of view is when someone bids by voice only. This can happen in a crowded room when from the back a bid is shouted out and the bidder cannot be seen. Usually, where the bidding is flowing smoothly and the level is well below the expected sale price the auctioneer will accept the bid and mark it as 'the voice'. Later on, if the bidder stays in the bidding pattern, at a suitable point when there is a lull, the auctioneer will ask the bidder to identify himself.

Another area of difficulty is where two bidders are sitting next to each other or directly one behind the other. Here it is important again to show clearly where the bid is. The simple solution is to say the name of the bidder if known, but when as is usually the case it is not known, then the bidder must be identified by referring to their sex and some item of dress. The objective is to reassure the bidder that the bid is with that person. This can simply be achieved by saying 'the gentleman in the yellow spotted tie' or 'the lady in the green dress centre row'.

At an auction of a lovely Georgian period Cotswold rectory for the Church Commissioners at the height of the property boom in the late 1980s the auction room was packed to capacity with standing room only. After completion of the formalities the bidding started and soon rose above the reserve price with fierce competition from six bidders who gradually as the price rose were reduced down to two people sitting next to each other three rows from the front. The auctioneer had identified them as the lady in the pink jacket and next to her the lady in the yellow dress. Taking the bids the auctioneer was saying 'on the pink' and 'on the yellow'. Now the bidding stopped and all thought that the pink bidder had secured the rectory, but as the hammer was raised for the first time a woman in the row directly behind the pink bidder, also wearing a pink cardigan bid! Promptly the auctioneer faced with an obvious dilemma had to come up with an identification which would not tongue tie him nor detract from the tempo of the bidding. The auctioneer pointing said 'The bidding is against you, front, the lady in the pink jacket. Your bid, madam, seated directly behind her wearing glasses.' Thank goodness she was wearing glasses! After more hectic bidding and several pauses the rectory was knocked down to an agent who made only one final bid.

A common practice of regular bidders at chattels auctions is to agree with the auctioneer a pattern of signals indicating their intent and the amount of the bid. The bidder hopes to achieve a degree of anonymity and a system of signals might be when the glasses are put on he is bidding and stops when they are removed. The practice while working reasonably well for chattels sales is not to be encouraged with real property auctions. In both scenarios the burden of remembering a variety of signals from several bidders can tax the most experienced auctioneer's memory to the limit in the heat of strong competitive bidding and all too easily mistakes can be made. Where such an arrangement is entered into between the auctioneer and a bidder and a mistake is made by the auctioneer, the burden of proof is upon the auctioneer where the interpretation of the signals from the bidder is incorrect, resulting in the bidder either failing to buy the lot or having the lot knocked down to him. It is considered that the auctioneer is probably likely to be held liable by the courts, because an authority has been accepted from the bidder by the auctioneer, knowing that in the heat of the auction sale there is inevitably a likelihood of misinterpretation.

The bidding pattern and its regulation

Several patterns of bidding have been mentioned in this chapter and to understand how this happens live in the room, the reader is urged to go along to as many auctions as possible to watch and listen to the style of the various auctioneers and the way in which they conduct their sales. It is interesting to note both their good and bad or weak points.

Regulating the bidding is the manner by which the auctioneer accepts the bids and adjusts the level of the increments. The art is to sense from the room and the attitude of the active participants whether or not they are content to go along with the increases set by the auctioneer and equally when a bidder seeks to change the level from say £1000 to £500 whether this is acceptable. As a general rule the initial steps will be high and then drop down gradually as the anticipated sale price is reached. For example on a lot worth £50,000 the auctioneer opens with a bid at £30,000 on behalf of his client and then invites increases of £5000 to which a bidder responds with a bid at £35,000 and so the bids go to £40,000. Now the auctioneer reduces the increases to £2000, genuine bids follow in sequence and nearing the reserve which has been set at £52,000, the auctioneer has to think ahead so as to place a genuine bid at £52,000. Assuming the latest bid is at £48,000 on the face of it the auctioneer only has to bid £50,000 and the bidder will be on the reserve at £52,000. However the bidder at £48,000 was obviously reluctant and possibly near his limit and therefore is unlikely to bid again. By dropping the increases at this point, to seasoned bidders this will indicate that the reserve price is near and possibly encourage a new bidder or the original one. At £1000 increases and bidding alternately for the client against genuine bidders the auctioneer can now reach the reserve on the correct step. Not all the pitfalls are yet crossed as the bidder might stop at £50,000 and the auctioneer is left with one bid at £51,000, or is he?

At this point the increases can be dropped to £500 and, again when coupled with some suitable comment, this underlines the fact that the reserve price is close by. Given only one genuine bidder the pattern will now take the auctioneer to the reserve at £52,000 with a genuine bid on that figure.

As with so many aspects of auctioneers' techniques, the handling of the bidding, coupled with the disclosure or otherwise of the reserve, is a matter of personal choice. Many prefer to avoid any comment which would indicate that the reserve is close, or even has been passed.

Watching various auctioneers in action it will be quickly noted that there are two distinct methods of conducting the bidding. The first method is for the auctioneer to say that the bidding will be taken in increments of a figure and to state the current bid. For example £47,000 on the blue tie, am I bid another £1000 anywhere? Thank you, Sir, £48,000 at the back left, against you at the front. £49,000 on the blue tie and now against you at the back left. This method makes it absolutely clear exactly at what level the bidding actually is and the increment sought.

Another method is for the auctioneer to invite the next bid by saying the desired figure. Here following the above example the selling pattern would be '£47,000 on the blue tie. £48,000 anywhere? Thank you, Sir, £48,000 at the back on the left. It is against you at the front, £49,000 am I bid?' This method to the uninitiated and nervous is confusing and often the auctioneer will be pulled up by someone asking during the bidding exactly what the bid is, especially remembering that given a run of bidding the auctioneer will be saying just the figure without preamble or follow on after it to indicate that it is a desired rather than actual bid figure. This style of conducting the bidding may be confusing, especially where those bidding are not familiar with auctions. It can lead to those present being uncertain as to the actual level of the bid, but for this style of bidding the auctioneer will make it absolutely clear whose bid it is and the figure which is being sought.

Whatever the style, the auctioneer must be completely flexible at all times. No two bidders will behave in exactly the same manner, and while one will be more than happy to proceed in advances of £1000, another will reach the same point but only with increases of £500.

Concluding the bidding

With the bidding for a particular lot nearly completed, the final challenge for the auctioneer is to ensure that the best possible final bid is achieved. For the inexperienced on the rostrum there is the temptation at the end of a long haul of bidding to breath a sigh of relief and bring the gavel down promptly on the final bid. Again the manner of finishing the sale will vary between the collective sale and the smaller auction. The auctioneer faced with a large number of lots will approach an individual lot on the basis that when it is offered to the room the bidders must clearly indicate that they are bidding and on the final bid there will be a slight pause with a comment such as 'Are you all done?' Then will follow the traditional words 'Selling for the first time, second time, third and final time', and then the gavel will fall.

By contrast with only a few lots to offer the auctioneer can afford the luxury of allowing sufficient time for the under bidder to reflect and possibly bid on. In country areas in the 1960s for cottages selling at around £5000 the last bidding increases were often in £10 units, whereas today they are in £50 units. The auctioneer will trot out the familiar phrases such as 'You have come a long way tonight, try another £50 and the property might be yours!' or 'While I chatter on have a word with your wife, another bid and you might succeed!' Following the last bid, to gain a few moments while the under bidder finally confirms that they can go no further, the auctioneer will cast around the room and confirm that any other bidders have finished. After that some more time can be gained by making comments about the lot and then back to the under bidder to see if there has been a change of heart. Especially with families bidding for a residential property, the likelihood is that given a chance to reflect they may make one or two more bids. One thing is certain that where a bidder shakes his head the auctioneer can never be certain that there is not another bid lying in that quarter!

In closing the bidding, once the auctioneer has satisfied him or herself that there are no more bids to be won from the company, they will now raise the gavel in a positive manner and say 'Are you all done, the bid at £77,500 is on the centre aisle to the gentleman in the green sports jacket. All done, I am selling, for the first time, pause, for the second time, pause, for the third and final time, sold.' The gavel comes down immediately and the contract is made between the buyer and the seller. As the fall of the gavel signifies the creation of the binding contract, the gavel must only be brought down at the conclusion of the auction of a lot, because this act is the sealing of the bargain between the buyer and the seller. The practice by some auctioneers of hitting the rostrum with the gavel three times is dangerous because if a bid was made after the first strike of the gavel, the contract has already been made and the later bid should not be accepted.

During the closing act of concluding the bidding the auctioneer and the clerk must closely examine the room to make certain that no-one has held back with the object of bidding at the last possible moment. This happens more often than might be imagined and in the highly charged atmosphere of the sale can be both dramatic and the cause of near heart failure for the auctioneer. It is not uncommon for the point to be reached of an apparent conclusion of the bidding with the gavel raised once or twice and then a late bid or bids to be made before the gavel finally falls for the third time.

The signing of the memorandum by both parties and the payment of the deposit immediately afterwards is the written record of the transaction created by the fall of the gavel. The auctioneer has the authority to sign the memorandum on behalf of both parties.

At the conclusion of the auction good manners dictate that the auctioneer thanks not only the vendor clients for entrusting their lots to his care but also the successful bidders and all those who have taken the time and trouble to attend at the sale.

The authority of the auctioneer in the room

While the auctioneer has wide powers vested in him or her the manner by which they are exercised are important. The legal issues in the practical context will be examined and through all the intricacies it is essential to maintain an authoritative approach with no aggravation and on an even handed basis to all involved. The authority is contained in the General Conditions of Sale and is preferably restated in the auction particulars.

The opening stages of the sale have already been covered in this chapter, but the auctioneer may be faced with a variety of situations during the bidding and these must be handled in a dignified and swift way. As with conducting the bidding here too the auctioneer has to be in complete control demonstrating both his authority, yet maintaining absolute politeness and never under any circumstances losing his or her temper nor appearing flustered. The pattern and flow of the bidding must not be lost but at the same time any dispute needs to be resolved promptly and authoritatively.

Disputed bids

This is the most common difficulty that faces the auctioneer and will arise where two people think that the bid is with them. The problem is often of the auctioneer's own making in that he or she has failed to identify clearly where the bidding lies. Quite simply the Conditions of Sale provide for this situation and a dispute may arise either during the bidding or on the fall of the hammer.

If the dispute occurs during bidding the solution is to stop momentarily and to identify clearly which bidder is being accepted. Then immediately to direct your attention to the person who has disputed where the bid lay and invite them to make the next bid. Now the bidding can continue with the auctioneer keeping a careful eye on the two parties! This situation frequently happens when bidders are sitting close to or behind one another. Here the usual gesture of an extended or pointing hand by the auctioneer does not indicate which party has the bid.

By contrast, when the dispute is made after the fall of the hammer, besides giving the auctioneer a nasty shock, there is an immediate situation to resolve. The question is whether or not the final bidder to whom the auctioneer brought down the hammer is the buyer. Again, the General Conditions of Sale are the source and guidance as to the correct course of action. Depending upon the drafting of the Conditions the wording usually takes the following form, 'In the event of any dispute in respect of the biding or other conduct at the auction the auctioneer's decision shall be final.' Another version is 'In the event of any dispute as to any bid, the Auctioneers may forthwith determine the dispute or put up the property again at the last undisputed bid or withdraw the property.'

As will be seen the Conditions of Sale provide the auctioneer with wide scope and when a dispute occurs on the fall of the hammer the auctioneer may consult with the clerk and if the situation is clear pronounce his decision immediately. Most auctioneers agree that if the hammer has fallen and the disputing party has made a late bid, then there is no reason to reopen the bidding. However, the situation is very different if the auctioneer or the clerk has missed that final bid since it has been made before the hammer fell. Practically the scene facing the auctioneer is likely to be open to some area of doubt and so extreme tact and a cool head is called for to resolve the dispute. Where the bidder has been overlooked, the lot should be put up again starting at the last bid to the person who made it. On the other hand, if the bid in the opinion of the auctioneer was made after the fall of the hammer it should be disallowed and the lot remain with the declared successful bidder.

While the purchaser will be well content with this decision, apart from the late bidder, the vendor client may not be so happy, as there will be the sense that the lot might have achieved a higher sale price. Without question the auctioneer should never be too hasty in closing the sale of a lot and ought always to cast around to draw out any reticent bidders before dropping the hammer.

The right to refuse bids

At first sight the refusal of a bid in the sale room may seem to be an unlikely occurrence, but it does happen. Situations arise where the auctioneer has reason to believe that the bidder will not honour the contract and complete. This might arise through personal experience at previous auctions of that individual or from reliable information obtained on the grapevine. Other likely reasons to refuse a bid are the behaviour of the person, perhaps they are intoxicated. One auctioneer who regularly sold small parcels of accommodation land acted for a delightful but eccentric client who liked to come along to the sales. Unfortunately, the client was not fully mentally capable and all the local auctioneers knew that in the excitement of the closing bidding he was inclined to join in. Imagine therefore the amusement when at a sale of an large estate by an auctioneer from outside the county a major parcel of land was knocked down to the client. Promptly the local auctioneer went up to the auctioneer and explained that the successful bidder not only had insufficient funds to complete but that it was likely that the deposit cheque would not be honoured. Furthermore, there were probably sufficient grounds for the bid to be held null and void on the grounds of mental incapacity. When approached the client smiled broadly and agreed that the unfortunate auctioneer had better reoffer the lot.

Relying on the Conditions of Sale the auctioneer has the right to refuse any bid without giving an explanation. The opinion is widely held that the auctioneer should not expand on the decision but should rather politely and firmly say that the bid is not accepted nor will any further bids from that person be taken. To start down the road of discussion in the open auction room is dangerous and could end in the individual having grounds for an action for defamation of character or worse!

The refusal of a bid may arise in the following circumstances:

1. The increase of the bid is not at the level as directed by the auctioneer. For example if the increases are running in £1000 units and a bid is made of £250 the auctioneer can refuse to accept it.

2. The final bid is below the reserve price.

3. The bidder does not have the necessary capability, authority or capacity. Here the auctioneer must have reasonable grounds to back up the decision as it is likely that the reason will have to be explained personally to the individual after the sale.

4. The bidder has a fiduciary relationship to the interested parties, perhaps a trustee of the vendor client who is bidding personally without having disclosed the intention to the auctioneer and the other trustees.

5. Bidding by third parties on behalf of the vendor when the right to bid has been reserved to the auctioneer *and* the auctioneer has specifically agreed with the vendor that no-one other than the auctioneer will bid in this capacity.

Withdrawn lots

As every auctioneer has experienced over the years on the rostrum, not every lot finds a buyer. Several points need to be watched for here, and the first is the manner by which the bidding on the lot is conducted. Remembering that the auctioneer can bid up to the reserve on behalf of the vendor, *but not at or above* the reserve, the question is, where in the bidding to withdraw the lot. Once the active bidding has stopped, usually the auctioneer will make one further bid on behalf of the vendor, provided that this lies below the reserve, and then announce that as the lot has failed to reach the reserve, it is withdrawn. The announcement will be followed by an invitation for anyone interested to come forward to the rostrum at the end of the sale to discuss a possible sale.

The question on the level of value at which to withdraw the lot is complex, because there is a desire to bring the bidding as close to the reserve as possible. This will indicate to anyone interested after the sale that there was genuine demand. The auctioneer will try therefore to bring the active bidding as close to the reserve as possible, but the ability to achieve this is strictly in the hands of those in the room. The reason is that the auctioneer must not take consecutive bids on behalf of the vendor. If the active bidding ceases, then only one bid above the last genuine bid can be made and the proceedings close with the lot being withdrawn because the reserve has not been achieved.

Finally, a vitally important point on withdrawing a real property lot is that the auctioneer *must not* bring the gavel down as this would signify the sealing of a contract.

14 After the Auction

Once the actual sale is finished the natural reaction is to relax, but the auctioneer's duties are not yet over. All the contracts or memorandums of sale have to be completed and any interest in the unsold lots handled.

The contracts

Each one must checked through to make certain that all the documentation which should be attached to them is in place. Any alterations must be initialled by both parties. Check that they are signed, dated, and that where appropriate the completion date is filled in, together with any other payments due on completion.

Deposit cheques

Again against each lot that has been sold, check that the hammer price agrees with the amount on the contract and that the deposit cheque represents 10% of the full purchase price.

The contracts, and sometimes the deposit cheques, are usually held by the vendor's solicitors. Frequently the auctioneer will hold the deposits.

In any event the cheques must be cleared by expedited banking clearance. Some auctioneers state in the Conditions of Sale that where the deposit cheques are cleared by the expedited procedure, the purchaser has to reimburse the vendor for the costs incurred.

Today the type of deposit cheque is usually stipulated and sometimes a personal cheque is not acceptable. The requirement is for a bankers' draft, a building society cheque or a cheque drawn on a solicitor's client account.

Credit cards are not accepted at property auction, but cash is!

Cash deposits

Although the payment of a deposit in cash is familiar to rural auctioneers, it is becoming increasingly common at major collective sales. This has reached a sufficient level to involve the use of security firms in handling the transfer of the large amounts of cash.

When cash deposits are paid there is the problem of forged notes. If all the money accepted for deposits is bundled up and subsequently some is declared to be forgeries, there is no way of identifying to which lot it relates. A suggested solution used by some auctioneers is to stamp every note with the lot number, or to bank each deposit separately.

Auctioneers need to be careful particularly when handling large sums of cash that they are satisfied their auction sale is not being used as a vehicle for laundering illegal sums of money. Under the Money Laundering Regulations 1993 any suspicious transactions must be reported to the police who will then make their own enquiries.

Insurance

The standard arrangement is for the purchaser to be liable for the insurance of the lot from the fall of the gavel. This is stated in the conditions of sale as a specific clause, and often it is overlooked by bidders.

Always point this out to buyers and where there might be a problem in the buyer effecting immediate cover, then by arrangement the vendor's solicitors may agree to hold cover for an agreed period, say 24 hours.

Value Added Tax

This is not chargeable on residential property. For commercial and investment lots the particulars usually contain a statement to the effect that purchasers must satisfy themselves as to whether or not VAT is chargeable on the purchase price by enquiry of the vendor's solicitors prior to the auction. Many catalogues today set out clearly in the description of the individual lots whether or not VAT is applicable.

Unsold lots

Assuming that the auctioneer has included in the terms of appointment the right to sell unsold lots in the room at or in advance of the reserve price, discussions can be conducted with any interested parties. While there is a temptation to jump at the first acceptable offer, always allow sufficient time for anyone else in the room to come forward. To outsiders it may come as something of a surprise to learn that a high proportion of unsold lots are successfully disposed of under binding contracts in this way.

On occasions the vendor will be present and their instruction can be taken as to whether or not they wish to sell and, if inclined towards a sale, the price.

Once a suitable buyer has been identified, and assuming that the necessary authority is in place, a binding contract can be entered into using the auction contract with the payment of the deposit.

Where lots remain unsold, then on return to the office all those who enquired about them must be informed as quickly as possible with a price guide that has been authorised by the vendor. Part of the appeal of auction sales is that the vendor has three bites of the cherry, because the auction contract enables a sale prior, a sale under the gavel and a sale after the auction to be successfully concluded. If unsold, the contract can still be used after the sale to secure a buyer without having to renegotiate the terms and conditions as with the protracted private treaty sale if the necessary authority is in place.

Subsequent events

The subsequent procedures and correspondence follow the pattern of private treaty sales, with the account for commission and agreed expenses being submitted to the vendor's solicitors a few days before the completion date. This account has to be approved and agreed by the vendor before the solicitor can pay it. Further points to note here are that, when the auctioneer holds the deposit, firstly, the agreement of both the vendor and purchaser should be obtained before it can be released, usually to the solicitor acting for the vendor.

Secondly, the interest on the deposit held in a client account must be accounted for when it has been held 'as agent for the vendor', or 'as agent for the purchaser' unless otherwise agreed. In the former case the interest is due to the vendor and the latter to the purchaser.

Where the deposit is held 'as stakeholder' the auctioneer is entitled to retain the interest. Unless otherwise instructed, the auctioneer will always hold the deposit as stakeholder. In such cases the deposit is held on trust for both parties and the auctioneer is entitled to retain the interest. The auctioneer will generally be asked to remit the deposit to the purchaser's solicitors as soon as the deposit cheque has been cleared.

Thirdly, if the commission and agreed expenses are to be deducted from the monies held, then the prior approval of the vendor to the account has to be obtained unless the appointment of the auctioneer specifically allows otherwise.

Once settled, it is usual to write and thank all parties involved in the sale. With regional and individual sales the purchasers will appreciate being sent a copy of the particulars and poster as a keepsake of the auction.

Auctioneer's commission and expenses

It is impossible categorically to give any firm guidance on the level of commission as there are wide-ranging variations for private treaty sales across the country, even when on a sole agency basis. There are also regional variations in the method of charging expenses, such as advertising and the erection of 'For Sale' boards.

As a broad rule of thumb in the south of England the agent's commission is inclusive of expenses on residential property with vacant possession, whereas from the midlands northwards, it is exclusive with the expenses charged separately. For all other categories of property the commission is usually exclusive of all expenses, irrespective of the location. Broadly speaking commission charges on residential property range from 1% to 3% on private treaty sales, and outside London the local rate may be increased by another ½% for auctions. From these comments it is clear that there are widely differing arrangements as between regions and individual auctioneers. Each vendor will agree at the outset the detailed basis of the fees and expenses.

With collective sales there may be a commission rate on the sale price plus expenses which under the Estate Agents Act 1979 must be itemised with any discounts obtained by the auctioneer being passed on to the vendor. Many auctioneers charge a Catalogue Entry Fee which covers all items of expenses; this obviates the necessity to provide a detailed breakdown under the Estate Agents Act 1979.

While it is dangerous to generalise, the expenses will lie in the range of ½% to 1½% of the anticipated sale price. However, much will depend upon whether or not the lot is included within a collective sale, where there are major cost savings in some areas, or offered as a single unit. Again the question of the extent of advertising, local or national, and the format and style of the auction particulars all have a direct bearing on the overall costs. Auction houses conducting regular collective sales routinely review and update their costings and are able to provide any intending vendor with an immediate indication of the auction costs including commission.

Post auction press release

Immediately after the auction a press release should be issued with the sale results. While the 'hammer price' is in the public domain and can be published, under no circumstances can the names of the vendors and purchasers be stated without their specific consents.

The same applies for the lots sold prior to the auction and here the sale price is also strictly confidential.

15 Moving Forward

The background

From the end of the Second World War the growth of London and provincial firms continued with little change over the next two decades. Business activity followed traditional and predictable patterns which had been established over the pre-war years. New technology was adopted as it became available, but few foresaw the major changes that would follow. This led in turn to firms seeking to broaden their base of activities and geographical coverage.

In the late 1950s the articled pupil route to qualification ended, although it was still possible to qualify by studying for the professional examinations through a correspondence course, today referred to as 'distance teaching'. Progressive, forward- looking firms were seeking to expand, and alongside there was a pool of young qualified men and women who were ambitious and determined not to be held back by the old style constraints of the established firms.

Another factor that played an important role was that partnerships relied for their continuity on the ability of incoming young people to pay substantial sums for goodwill which in turn provided retiring partners with a lump sum on leaving the firm. The problem which faced the senior partners by the late 1960s was that those forward thinking and entrepreneurial men were married with young families and home owners. Their borrowing abilities were nil or close to it, and therefore new devices had to be created to finance firms. Routes into a partnership began to be eased by provision of pension plans for those facing retirement, separating working and property capital, and the elimination of goodwill; after all whoever in their right mind would wish to buy a firm of auctioneers! While the professional bodies fought a long rearguard action against firms becoming limited liability companies, the writing was on the wall that this was the inevitable outcome as a preferred choice for some.

With the advent of the motorway network, intercity high speed trains and modern telecommunication systems, the overall effect was that clients no longer needed to be on the doorstep and in parallel they were demanding a more sophisticated level of service. In the commercial, retail and investment markets the local freehold interests rapidly passed out of local ownership into the hands of national and international companies, leading to a steady erosion of the provincial firms' client base.

London surveyors and those in major provincial centres began to expand, both in the make-up of their staff and by establishing regional offices, often by acquisition of existing businesses. Commercially based regional firms actively stamped their influence on regions and sought out contacts and reciprocal arrangements with London practices. Residential firms established branch networks in order to dominate a city or county.

From 1970 to the early 1980s major role players emerged on a national and international basis as well as those working regionally. However, a major sea-change was about to alter the face of agency and property auctioneering firms. Simply, it was the sudden realisation that goodwill had reappeared and that third parties were not only prepared, but also competing, to acquire firms – these being the financial institutions.

Following a long-fought campaign for freedom to compete with each other on a level playing field, the clearing banks and building societies, anxious to rapidly expand their client base and range of income-producing services, were freed of constraints by deregulation in 1981 to enter the fields of agency and insurance amongst a whole range of activities. This was achieved mainly through acquisition, and many agency firms were quick to realise the benefit of cashing up their businesses with the partners continuing as salaried employees. The first sale of a firm was to Lloyds Bank in 1984, and within a period of a few years many building societies and insurance companies had purchased estate agents, creating chains of offices across the country. Exactly how many billions of pounds were poured into these new ventures has never been stated. A 'guestimate' is that in the order of £2½ billion was spent.

The effect on the property auctioneering scene was predictable. Many long established firms ceased to exist and in the process of rebranding property auctioneering was a long way down the list of priorities. Alongside all this, a high percentage of the senior partners chose retirement, immediately or after a few years, and with them departed not just the well-known individual, but also the hundreds of years of experience which had filtered down the successive generations of auctioneers in that practice.

During the boom period of the late 1980s leading up to the recession that was to follow, upgrading of portfolios by institutional investors from smaller investments to larger sized parcels led to a large number of portfolio sales. A rising market gave the entrepreneurial property companies the chance to acquire new portfolios on a wholesale volume basis, and to trade out single investment lots at a considerable profit. The auction room was the exit route as it could handle the volume and provide a clear timescale. The residential volume sales, many with vacant possession, only followed some 3 to 4 years later once the downturn took hold. The rise of the London auction market was led by the commercial and investment market with the residential volume sales coming afterwards.

At the end of the 1980s the recession began to bite and continued into the early 1990s. What began with a few estate agency office closures soon changed gear into the wholesale closure of groups of offices or disposals at token prices in many cases. With the combined effect of these closures and the apparent lack of regional auctioneers, London auction houses were quick to spot the gap in the market place, and went on to achieve domination, acting for banks, finance houses, building societies, liquidators and receivers on sales of repossessed properties and businesses in financial difficulty.

From less than 5000 repossessed homes in 1980 the figure peaked in 1987 at over 25,000, and then after a decline over the next two years it rose again to just below 45,000 in 1990.

Eventually, several regional firms won a slice of this business, and with a decreasing rate of repossessions the challenge for all auctioneers is to generate a sufficient volume of lots for their collective sales. Experiments have been made with regional auctions and eyes cast towards the European market place. Without question the major auction houses have established a commanding position in the property market for commercial, industrial, retail and investment property. On the residential side the picture is more complex and interestingly throughout recent years none of the national names associated with handling country estates and houses has entered the scene with a view to creating a London auction centre devoted to this type of property.

As Owen Bevan states in his Preface to *Marketing and Property People*: 'The commercial market is increasingly polarising into a relatively small number of international megafirms, well established and well positioned in major UK cities to attract prestige instructions, closely followed by a small number of large UK firms, well presented in the provinces. In addition to these is a diminishing number of established regional firms and the main mass of the professions practising in groups of up to five partners.'

Recent technological and information innovations

The Jones Lang Wootton Auction Results Analysis System (ARAS), launched in 1992, analyses the current market and its trends, providing an extremely valuable source of verifiable data to the commercial property market. Regular reports and statistics on ARAS appear in all the major property publications and they make for extremely interesting reading.

AuctionCall provided by *EG Faxwise* provides dedicated premium lines for auction houses to enable the public to access direct a range of services including Catalogue Request Lines, Instant Fax Service for catalogues, price guides, addendum and sale results. Telephone Information Service on an interactive voice response basis for price guides, addendum and sale results is also available.

A recent innovation is the launch of a TV and cable satellite station dedicated to the non-stop coverage of auctions. The aim, according to Trojan TV, is for a seven days a week service. They hope to cover 800 sales a year, worldwide, including coverage of all types of auctions.

In 1993 'Live Link' was launched by *EG Faxwise* to link the public to the auction room by dialling up a special number at the start of the sale with the proceedings being relayed live to the callers.

Figure 15.1 Advertisements from *Estates Gazette* show the range of information services available today (Reproduced with permission).

Faxwise, a private venture in conjunction with Estates Gazette, began development in 1992 of a database of auction sales and this was launched in 1995 as *EG Datawise* with listings of over 46,000 lots sold over the previous 5 years through London auction houses. By the end of 1997 the records had been extended to 90,000 lots and the database for selected lots back to 1991. Shortly the database will go back to 1982 as the point for index linked computations of Capital Gains Tax calculations. In the March 1998 Budget amendments to the basis for the calculation of capital gains means that effectively the date was frozen at April 1998 and index linked computations will only apply in future between 1982 and 1998 as appropriate. A further extension of the service is the inclusion of every property auction in the country with regular returns from 75 firms conducting sales. The database can be accessed via computer, or the Internet.

A new service launched in August 1997 by *EG Datawise*; known as 'AuctionWatch', it is aimed at those seeking property. By using fax or the post agents are able to maintain an up-to-date listing of their properties, including full particulars, photographs and plans, and the public may search by geographical area and type. The levels of access and information available to the public is at the absolute discretion of the participating agent.

Information Technology manifests itself in many forms and accessibility to one and all can present pitfalls for the unwary. It will be interesting to see how the role of the Internet develops as a communication channel, a marketing tool and a database. The major hurdles for the Internet are speed of response and accessibility, not only by each business, but also every household. As yet an auctioneer cannot afford to rely solely on one system of communication. New systems and methods of communication are continually evolving, all of which need to be closely monitored as to their effective impact on the various aspects of the business, the clients and the public.

The landed professions

Brief reference was made in Chapter 1 to the historical background of the landed professional bodies. It is interesting to read in the various journals that once again the idea of a merger of the two senior ones, namely The Royal Institution of Chartered Surveyors, current membership 73,500, and The Incorporated Society of Valuers & Auctioneers, current membership 7000, is under discussion. A merger was nearly achieved in 1989, but RICS failed to achieve the necessary number of votes in favour. Today, the proposal is again on the agenda with the attendant well-worn letters appearing in the journals. Perhaps events have now moved on to enable all those involved to adopt a broader view and, most importantly of all, to place their clients and the property market ahead of internal politics. In the world outside of the landed professions it does not make sense to have two bodies representing this vital element of advice, when most other aspects speak with a single voice. What all members of RICS and ISVA have to bear in mind is that there are other professions and advisers inextricably linked to, and involved in, property transactions on a day-to-day basis who are only too anxious to steal a march by encroaching into the domain of the valuer, surveyor and auctioneer.

Looking forward

However, the picture does not end here as we live in changing times, especially in the attitude towards consumer protection and what is described in some quarters as 'The Nanny State'. It is not inconceivable that the rule of *caveat emptor* in property transactions will be eroded to the point of extinction within the next decade. Today, the auctioneer is at the stage where there must be absolute transparency of all information provided, plus detailed file records of the sources and checks which have been made to verify the statements in the particulars. Property auctioneers have always rightly taken pride in the fact that, whatever the form and guise of new legislation, they have little or no difficulty in complying. Simply whatever is required of them, in the main is already part of their standard procedures.

To meet this challenge today's auction house must take on board an increasingly open and friendly manner, recognising that both the client base and the buying-public need to be educated in the art of auction, be reassured and provided with an ever growing amount of information and practical assistance in advance of the sale date. This means bringing into the process not only solicitors and surveyors, but also financial advisers and specialist contractors to create the total unbiased package from Day 1 of the marketing of the lot. Alongside, auction houses increasingly run auction seminars and provide information packs on the subject. This activity will become commonplace and in the interests of all should be extended to every firm of auctioneers. Auctions can show private treaty sales a route to greater efficiency by stressing 'vendor preparation' as a prerequisite to a smooth and less stressful transaction.

Duncan Moir writing in the *Estates Gazette*, 9 August 1997, on auctions says 'More than 4 billion pounds of real estate has gone under the hammer in London since 1991, a volume of business that cannot be dismissed easily. At the risk of being seen to protest too much, as an auctioneer I am anxious to convince the "non-believers" that the efficiency and transparency of these transactions go a long way toward underpinning the activities of the wider investment market.' Later in the leader article he goes on to say 'Many auction houses have worked hard to inform buyers and to make the auction room less daunting to newcomers. This has extended the profile of auctions from a wholesale "dealer-driven" market into a retail, private-investor market.'

He concludes his article with the telling commentary: 'It is ironic that the property industry's most public display of market activity is one of the least-understood routes available to both advisers and principals. The auction room is now a more comfortable environment for all purchasers, and forms one of the pillars of our industry. It provides a sophisticated marketplace in which the newcomer, as well as the entrepreneur, can flourish.'

Currently, there are no statistics on the number of property auctioneers in the UK, nor on the number of firms and their geographical spread. Inevitably media coverage concentrates on the London scene which tends to give not only the public, but also fellow professional advisers, the impression that west of Slough and north of Watford little happens. No doubt the day will arrive when it is possible to obtain a clearer overall picture on a national basis. Certainly property auctions are regularly staged throughout the UK in most major regional centres by locally established auctioneers. Additionally, several of the main national property auctioneers conduct sales outside London and a few conduct auctions at multi-centre locations. This involves holding sales over a series of days in cities spread across the country. For researchers of this subject the challenge is to obtain accurate information on a national footing.

Everyone agreed that 1995 was a year best forgotten, with capital realised under the hammer down by almost a third on 1994 for the top 12 London firms, the average lot achieving £170,000 as compared with £220,000 in 1994 (ARAS). Over the same period the number of lots offered fell by 10%. By contrast, reporting in the *Estates Gazette* on 18 January 1997, ARAS confirmed that 1996 was the best year for auctions since the boom of the 1980s. In spite of fewer lots being offered, more were sold and for more money. Whereas in 1995 £148 million was realised under the hammer, in 1996 the figure rose substantially to £252 million.

A year later saw ARAS reporting in the *Estates Gazette* on 24 January 1998 that £405 million of property was sold by auction, an increase of 61% on the previous year. Richard Auterac of Jones Lang Wootton also reported that the number of lots offered had increased to 2384, 42% up on 1996, and only two lots short of the record of 2386 set in 1989.

While property auctioneers seek to work to a rule of thumb of 80% to 90% as the success rate for sales under the gavel, the achievement of an overall figure in 1996 and 1997 at 77% was impressive. Richard Auterac concludes his report with the telling remarks: 'The market for auction services will continue to grow in terms of volumes selling in the market because, over the next 12-18 months, investors will want to take a profit and auction may be the principal way of accessing the buyers of tomorrow.'

Little has been written on the role that women have played and will increasingly play in the property auctioneering scene. While they are an increasingly familiar sight on the rostrum at chattels sales, the same is yet to be seen with real property auctions. An article in *The Valuer*, the journal of ISVA, in October 1995 discussed the question of why female auctioneers are almost unknown, and yet they hold senior roles in leading chattels auction houses. The writer pondered the question as to whether they found the world of fine art more glamorous and more easily attuned to that environment. The time will come, sooner rather than later, when a female property auctioneer will command the rostrum, but like their male counterparts the route is perhaps an even more frustrating one than a decade ago with fewer property auction houses today, and correspondingly fewer openings. By the 1990s women had eclipsed the make-up of staff in the typical 'High Street' residential estate agent's office and it is logical that the breadth of their experience and expertise should extend to the rostrum.

Property auctioneers will continue to follow their traditional role in the market place in all sectors. The challenge is whether the continued education of the client base can result in a wider acceptance of auction as the preferred method of sale and purchase. In order to maintain the necessary volume of lots coming under the hammer, and in turn support the overheads of a high profile auction department, the leading auction houses are actively casting around for new avenues to bring in fresh sources of instructions. Great strides have been made in recent years to make auctions more 'user friendly', and with continuing innovations in high-technology information systems there will have to be experimentation and capital investment, some of which inevitably will fall on stony ground. While there is an attitude still prevalent in this country to leave others to try out new ideas and to gloat on their misfortune when they do not succeed, it is only by innovation that expanded and new market places are opened up. To witness a major Canadian livestock auctioneer selling stock on ranches scattered over many thousands of square miles seated behind his office desk and linked to the ranches and buyers by satellite was amazing. Remembering the historical attitude of both buyers and sellers to livestock auctions, it would be reasonable to assume that this area of auctioneering activity would be last to move to this remote high-tech system, divorced from the intimacy and social atmosphere.

The current Government-led proposals to try and reform the minefield of buying and selling homes has already stirred a group of solicitors in England and Wales to move into residential estate agency on a similar basis to their Scottish brethren. Perhaps this may goad local estate agents to reconsider the merits of more actively promoting auctions, as one of a number of countermeasures against this intrusion into their market place. However, if this is to be achieved, the landed professions and the educational institutions will have to provide a far greater understanding of the role of auctions and their mechanics for their students.

The Focus '97 article on Auctions in the 13 December 1997 issue of the *Estates Gazette* quoted Gary Murphy of Allsop & Co as predicting that auction rooms during 1998 will benefit from more business from housing associations, as well as from the guaranteed exit route BES (Business Expansion Scheme) companies. 'This market is titanic – it's huge. There is a tidal wave of investment stock about to hit the market and an almost limitless number of buyers waiting to absorb it. There will be so much activity next year in the residential sector. It is, without doubt, the biggest growth sector of the property market.'

As a measure of widening the net of vendors several auctioneers have experimented with 'conditional auction contracts' which has not received the support of most auctioneers. This is where the vendor has a period of time after the auction when the final bid can be accepted or declined, but the bidder cannot withdraw, and so is locked in.

Another practice has been to include within the Conditions of Sale the right for the auctioneer on behalf of the vendor 'to bid up to *and above* the reserve price'. This practice, while understandable on the vendor's part, is definitely not in the spirit and tradition of the auction, and more importantly may prompt those interested in protecting the interests of consumers to question this clause. After all, those auction houses adopting this approach already have another route open to them, namely to adopt a discretionary reserve.

It is reassuring to note that RICS, ISVA and NAEA are jointly launching an updated set of Guidance Notes for Property Auctioneers. Richard Auterac, chairman of the RICS Property Auctioneering Panel, says that the aim has been to ensure a consistent approach to the conduct of property auctions by encapsulating best practice and ensuring that entrants to the market comply with the rules. He goes on to say that people's perception of auctioneering is dominated by the chattels, cattle and car auctions, and perhaps the one-off auctions above a pub. We have a big PR job to do. Auctioneers have traditionally been very conservative in their approach to marketing, and we need to demonstrate to the wider world that the job of property auctioneering is done very professionally. He sees the new notes as part of a wider process of opening up the property auction market to new groups of buyers and sellers.

Another interesting move which has the backing of RICS is the attempt to establish a new set of Conditions of Sale for property being sold by auction. This is an extremely complex exercise, but one which, if achieved, will considerably enhance the standing of auctions.

As auctioneers look forward to the new century all accept that change is certain, but are determined to retain the standards of excellence so jealously built up by the generations that preceded them. With the increasing awareness of consumer protection in its widest sense, a measure of care must be achieved to ensure that with the steady drip-feed of legislation the pendulum does not swing too far the other way. Working property auctioneers and their representative bodies need to be ever vigilant to protect not only their own interests, but in the broader long term view those of their clients and the general public.

Appendix A

The following *Guidance Notes for Auctioneers Proposing to Sell Real Estate at Auction in England and Wales* are reproduced by permission of The Royal Institution of Chartered Surveyors which owns the copyright.

1 Legal Responsibilities

1.1 The Law

Auctioneers, vendors and purchasers should appreciate that a considerable amount of the practice of offering property for sale, whether by private treaty or by auction, is regulated by law. The Auctioneer's legal and professional responsibilities are defined particularly in:

- Auctioneers Act 1845

- Sale of Land by Auction Act 1867

- Auction (Bidding Agreements) Acts 1927 and 1969

- Misrepresentation Act 1967

- Sale of Goods Act 1979

- Estate Agents Act 1979 and Regulations and any Orders made thereafter

- Landlord and Tenant Act 1987

- Property Misdescriptions Act 1991 and any Orders made thereunder

- Money Laundering Regulations 1993

- Unfair Terms in Consumer Contracts Regulations 1994

- Housing Act 1996

1.2 Personal Interest

Under the provisions of the Estate Agents Act 1979 it is the Auctioneer's duty to notify both vendor and prospective purchasers of any personal interests and the Auctioneer must be aware that the definition of 'personal interest' in the Act is wide.

2   Pre-Auction

2.1   Terms of Engagement

2.1.1   The Estate Agents Act 1979, and the statutory instruments made under it, regulate the manner in which all estate agents have to notify their fees. The precise terms of the Auctioneer's appointment should be agreed in writing and any such terms must include:

(a) definition of the Auctioneer's basis of appointment and if the terms sole agent, joint agent or sole selling rights are used, the statutory wording must be incorporated;

(b) the vendor's liability for fees and expenses (to include sales that may be effected prior or subsequent to auction) specifying precisely under what circumstances the liability will arise, the amount of the fees and expenses and the duration of the period of appointment;

(c) the vendor's liability for fees and expenses in the event of the vendor withdrawing instructions between appointment and the auction date;

(d) the rights of the Auctioneer to deduct agreed fees and expenses from the deposit held; and

(e) the Auctioneer's responsibility and procedure for the reporting of bids prior to the auction.

2.1.2   Additionally it should include:

(a) the manner in which the Auctioneer may accept deposits, including by cheque and banker's draft;

(b) whether the deposit will be held as stakeholder or agent for the vendor or the purchaser and to whom any interest earned on that deposit accrues, and to whom the balance of the deposit moneys shall be sent;

(c) the extent of the Auctioneer's right:

(i)   to refuse bids;
(ii) to determine disputes between bidders;
(iii) to regulate bidding increments;

(iv) to accept postal, telephone, telex or facsimile bids by way of proxy (with appropriate indemnities from the vendor and the bidder in the event of a failure of communications);

(v) to release any bidder acting as agent from personal liability;

(vi) to bid on behalf of the vendor and to advise the vendor not to bid. It is strongly recommended that the Auctioneer does not accept instructions where the vendor requires the right to bid the reserve or over the reserve;

(d) the Auctioneer's responsibility and procedure for inspections;

(e) the Auctioneer's right to instruct the vendor's solicitor to undertake all local and other searches and provide special conditions of sale and to make all relevant legal documentation available to prospective purchasers;

(f) confirmation from the vendor that any existing instructions to other agents have been withdrawn (excepting those acting as Joint Auctioneers). If Joint Auctioneers are appointed it is advisable for the Auctioneer to ensure that the duties and liabilities of the Joint Auctioneer are documented and the basis of remuneration and reimbursement of costs has been agreed;

(g) the Auctioneer's right to change the venue or date of the auction at his discretion;

(h) as the Auctioneer does not have implied authority to sell prior or post-auction, the circumstances in which the auctioneer is authorised to sign the Memorandum of Sale on behalf of the vendor; and

(i) a warranty that information supplied to the Auctioneer by the vendor or the vendor's solicitor or the vendor's managing agents is accurate and an indemnity against liability for inaccuracy.

2.2   Material Matters which may Affect the Sale

2.2.1   The Auctioneer should ask to be notified by the vendor and/or the solicitors of public health notices, local land charges, financial changes, major arrears of rent, disputes and material matters relating to the property being offered for sale.

2.3   Provision of Legal Documentation and Other Legal Issues

2.3.1   All relevant documents and plans relating to the property being sold should be available for inspection at the offices of the Auctioneer or the vendor's solicitors for as long a period as possible prior to the sale and in the auction room.

2.3.2   It may be helpful for the solicitor acting for the vendor to attend at the auction to facilitate and explain queries which may be raised of a legal nature or pertaining to the legal documentation.

2.3.3   The General Condition of Sale, Memorandum of Sale and any notices to bidders are usually published by the Auctioneer and regulate the conduct of the sale and other matters which apply to all the lots in the auction; the Special Conditions of Sale are usually prepared by the vendor's solicitor which apply usually to a specific lot.

2.4   Auction Venue

2.4.1   The Auctioneer should check that:

(a) there is no prohibition against holding an auction on the property;

(b) the permitted size of the auction room will accommodate the bidders and, in particular, that the fire regulations will be complied with;

(c) the insurance cover maintained by the hirers of the auction room is satisfactory; and

(d) any local authority regulations that may exist can be complied with.

2.5   Sale Boards

2.5.1   The Auctioneer should not erect a sale board without the vendor's consent.

2.5.2   The Auctioneer must comply with the relevant planning regulations for the erection of the boards and should require sign-board erectors to carry satisfactory and sufficient insurance.

2.5.3   Auctioneers should, if appropriate, either directly or through the vendor, consult beforehand with the occupier and/or the landlord of the property upon which the board is to be erected.

2.5.4   The Auctioneer should arrange for the board to be removed from the property after the auction and the board erectors required to make good all damage to the property.

2.6   Price Guides

2.6.1   If price guides are given they should not be misleading. It is helpful for prospective purchasers if the Auctioneer defines the basis of the price guide, for example, 'the vendor's initial expectation of the level of the reserve'.

2.6.2   For the benefit of prospective purchasers reference should be made in the catalogue that price guides may be subject to adjustment, where appropriate, in the lead up to the auction.

2.6.3   The Auctioneer should make reasonable endeavours to contact all known interested parties who have specifically registered their interest and advise them of any adjustment in the price guide. However, it should be drawn to the attention of prospective purchasers that it is their responsibility to make regular contact with the auctioneers to establish whether there has been any adjustment in the price guide.

2.7   Reserve Price

2.7.1   It is usual for the reserve price to be fixed prior to the auction day. This is the figure below which the Auctioneer is not authorised to sell at auction.

2.7.2   It is good practice for the Auctioneer to confirm in writing the reserve price.

2.7.3   Any reserve price will remain strictly confidential to the Auctioneer, his staff and the vendor and the Auctioneer will not disclose reserve prices to any third parties unless instructed to do so by the vendor. Only with the agreement of the vendor will a reserve price be disclosed in the catalogue or at the auction.

2.7.4   The existence, but not the amount, of the reserve should be disclosed in the General Conditions of Sale with an indication of the Auctioneer's right to bid on behalf of the vendor up to, but not at or above, the reserve price.

2.8.   Sales Prior to the Auction

2.8.1   The Auctioneer should ask to be notified by the vendor of any sale contemplated by the vendor prior to the auction.

2.8.2   The Auctioneer should make it clear to prospective purchasers in the auction catalogue that there is always the possibility of the vendor selling at any time before the auction and that prospective purchasers should verify the availability of the lot immediately prior to the auction.

2.8.3   If the property is sold or withdrawn prior to the auction, the Auctioneer should use reasonable endeavours to notify all known interested parties who have specifically registered interest. However, it should be drawn to the attention of the prospective purchasers that it is their responsibility to make regular contact with he auctioneer to establish whether the property has been sold or withdrawn prior to the auction.

2.9.   Value Added Tax (VAT)

2.91.   The auctioneer should request the vendor to confirm whether or not the sale is subject to VAT and prospective purchaser should be made aware of this.

2.9.2   It is advisable for the auctioneers to request the vendor to give clear written instructions on the treatment of VAT on the deposit moneys.

2.10   Joint Auctioneers

2.10.1   If there is a Joint auctioneer his duties, responsibilities and terms of appointment need to be approved by the vendor.

3   Auction Catalogue

3.1   The Particulars

3.1.1   The Auctioneer should appreciate that auction particulars have to be factual, accurate and comply with the Property Misdescriptions Act 1991 and all relevant statutory instruments. It is recommended that Auctioneers forward proofs of auction particulars to the vendor and the solicitors and managing agents (if appropriate) for verification.

3.1.2   The auction particulars may form part of the contract unless specifically excluded by the Conditions of Sale. Notwithstanding any purported exclusion, the auction particulars may be deemed to be part of the contract or to constitute representations with respect to the property.

3.1.3   Catalogues frequently incorporate the General and Special Conditions of Sale and the Memorandum of Sale but, if they are not included, the catalogue should indicate their existence and where and when they are available for inspection prior to the sale. A buyer who is not given effective notice of Conditions of Sale may be able to challenge the applicability of those Conditions of Sale to the contract.

3.1.4   Matters relating to the conduct of the auction should be stated in the catalogue or reserved in the General Conditions of Sale. The Conditions should also contain the right of the Auctioneer to:

(a) sell as a whole or in lots;

(b) amend the lotting order;

(c) withdraw or sell the property prior to the auction;

(d) determine the conduct of the auction and any disputes between competing bidders;

(e) regulate the size of bidding increments;

(f) refuse bids; and

(g) bid on behalf of the vendor.

3.2   Plans and Photographs

3.2.1   Plans are frequently included in the catalogue for location and identification purposes only. Copyright consents must be obtained. Photographs and plans should not be misleading and must be as up to date as is reasonably possible.

3.2.2   The Auctioneer should request the vendor and the solicitors to verify the accuracy of the site plans included in the catalogue.

4   The Auction

4.1   Amendments and Variations

4.1.1   The Auctioneer should bring to the attention of prospective purchasers prior to auction any material variations, alterations or amendments to the particulars or Conditions of Sale of which they are aware that may have arisen in the lead-up period to the auction. Any amendments affecting the contract for the sale of the property should be contained within an addendum and made available to all prospective bidders at the commence-ment of the auction. It is advisable to attach the addendum to the Memorandum of Sale.

4.1.2   If the Auctioneer is selling subject to an addendum, it is helpful to bidders for the Auctioneer to remind them of this before each lot.

4.2.   Auction (Bidding Agreements) Acts 1927 and 1969

4.2.1   It is a statutory requirement that the respective extracts of these Acts be clearly displayed together with the full name and address of the Auctioneer.

4.3   Telephone and Proxy Bids

4.3.1   It is advisable for any telephone or proxy bids to be governed by terms which are set out in writing and signed by the bidder. These should include an exclusion of liability on the part of the auctioneer in the event of telephone failure. The procedures proposed for receiving deposits in respect of telephone and commission bids need to be clearly understood and agreed by both vendor and bidder.

4.3.2   Telephone or proxy bidders should be made aware that it is their responsibility to enquire of the Auctioneer immediately prior to the sale, whether there have been any material variations, alterations or amendments to the particulars or Conditions of Sale.

4.4   Responsibility to Insure

4.4.1   If it is to be the responsibility of the purchaser to insure the property on the fall of he gavel, it is advisable for this to be brought to the attention of prospective purchasers in the Conditions of Sale.

4.5   Payment of the Deposit and Completion of the Memorandum by the Successful Purchaser

4.5.1   It is helpful to the prospective purchasers to have included in the catalogue and repeated at the start of the auction by the Auctioneer an explanation of the procedures for the payment of the deposit and the completion of the Memorandum of Sale.

4.5.2   The Conditions of Sale should state whether the deposit is received by the Auctioneer as agent for the vendor, or as stakeholder.

4.6   Unsold Lots

4.6.1   Where a lot fails to reach the reserve price the Auctioneer should:

(a) state that it has not be sold;

(b) not bring the gavel down; and

(c) prior to withdrawing the lot as unsold, not use inappropriate phraseology which gives the impression that the bidding is at or above the reserve price.

4.7   Conduct of the Auction

4.7.1   To avoid later disputes it is advisable for the Auctioneer to clearly indicate who is the highest bidder before bringing down the gavel.

4.7.2   It is usual for the Auctioneer to have a clerk whose responsibility is to record the bids in case there is a later dispute. Some Auctioneers make a sound recording of the auction proceedings as well.

4.7.3   The Auctioneer must make reasonable efforts to ensure that the successful bidder signs the Memorandum and pays the deposit money at the auction.

5   Post-Auction

5.1   Publication of Auction Results

5.1.1   Published results must be accurate. When a property is sold prior to or post-auction it is usual not to publish the sale price without the vendor's and purchaser's consents.

5.1.2   The identity of the vendor or purchaser should not be disclosed without their consent.

5.1.3   If notices under the Housing Act 1996 have been served prior to the auction the Auctioneer is advised to take legal advice prior to selling post-auction.

Appendix B

The following extracts from Statutes included in Appendices B-E are reproduced with the permission of the Controller of Her Majesty's Stationery Office.

AUCTIONEERS ACT 1845

...

Auctioneer, before he shall commence any Sale, shall suspend or affix a Ticket or Board containing his full Christian and Surname and Place of Residence

VII. And be it enacted, That every Auctioneer, before beginning any Auction, shall affix or suspend, or cause to be affixed or suspended, a Ticket or Board containing his true and full Christian and Surname and Residence painted, printed, or written in large Letters publicly visible and legible in some conspicuous Part of the Room or Place where the auction is held, so that all Persons may easily read the same, and shall also keep such Ticket or Board so affixed or suspended during the whole Time of such Auction being held; and if any Auctioneer begins any Auction, or acts as Auctioneer at any Auction, in any Room or Place where his Name and Residence is not so painted or written on a Ticket or Board so affixed or suspended, and kept affixed or suspended as aforesaid, he shall forfeit for every such Offence the Sum of Twenty Pounds.

...

Appendix C

SALE OF LAND BY AUCTION ACT 1867

...

Interpretation of Terms

3. 'Auctioneer shall mean any Person selling by Public Auction any Land, whether in Lots or otherwise:
    'Land' shall mean any Interest in any Messuages, Lands, Tenements, or Hereditaments of whatever Tenure:
    'Agent' shall mean the Solicitor, Steward, or Land Agent of the Seller:
    'Puffer' shall mean a Person appointed to bid on the Part of the Owner.

Where Sales are Invalid in Law to be also invalid in Equity

4. 'And whereas there is at present a Conflict between Her Majesty's Courts of Law and Equity in respect of the Validity of Sales by Auction of Land where a Puffer has bid, although no Right of bidding on behalf of the Owner was reserved, the Courts of Law holding that all such Sales are absolutely illegal, and the Courts of Equity under some Circumstances giving effect to them, but even in Courts of Equity the Rule is unsettled: And whereas it is expedient that an End shall be put to such conflicting and unsettled Opinions:' Be it therefore enacted, That from and after the passing of this Act whenever a Sale by Auction of Land would be invalid at Law by reason of the Employment of a Puffer, the same shall be deemed invalid in Equity as well as at Law.

Rule respecting Sale without Reserve, &c

5. 'And whereas as Sales of Land by Auction are now conducted many of such Sales are illegal, and could not be enforced against an unwilling Purchaser, and it is expedient for the Safety of both Seller and Purchaser that such Sales should be so conducted as to be binding on both Parties:' Be it therefore enacted by the Authority aforesaid as follows: That the Particulars or Conditions of Sale by Auction of any Land shall state whether such Land will be sold without Reserve, or subject to a reserved Price, or whether a Right to bid is reserved; if it is stated that such Land will be sold without Reserve, or to that Effect, then it shall not be lawful for the Seller to employ any Person to bid at such Sale, or for the Auctioneer to take knowingly any Bidding from any such Person.

Rule respecting Sale subject to Right of Seller to bid as he may think proper

6. And where any Sale by Auction of Land is declared either in the Particulars or Conditions of such Sale to be subject to a Right for the Seller to bid, it shall be lawful for the Seller or any One Person on his Behalf to bid at such Auction in such Manner as he may think proper.

...

Appendix D

AUCTIONS (BIDDING AGREEMENTS) ACT 1927

Certain bidding agreements to be illegal

1. (1) If any dealer agrees to give, or gives, or offers any gift or consideration to any other person as an inducement or reward for abstaining, or for having

abstained, from bidding at a sale by auction either generally or for any particular lot, or if any person agrees to accept, or accepts, or attempts to obtain from any dealer any such gift or consideration as aforesaid, he shall be guilty of an offence under this Act, and shall be liable on summary conviction to a fine not exceeding one hundred pounds, or to a term of imprisonment for any period not exceeding six months, or to both such fine and such imprisonment:

Provided that, where it is proved that a dealer has previously to an auction entered into an agreement in writing with one or more persons to purchase goods at the auction bona fide on a joint account and has before the goods were purchased at the auction deposited a copy of the agreement with the auctioneer, such an agreement shall not be treated as an agreement made in contravention of this section.

(2) For the purposes of this section the expression 'dealer' means a person who in the normal course of his business attends sales by auction for the purpose of purchasing goods with a view to reselling them.

(3) In England and Wales a prosecution for an offence under this section shall not be instituted without the consent of the Attorney-General or the Solicitor-General.

Right of vendors to treat certain sales as fraudulent

2. Any sale at an auction, with respect to which any such agreement or transaction as aforesaid has been made or effected, and which has been the subject of a prosecution and conviction, may, as against a purchaser who has been a party to such agreement or transaction, be treated by the vendor as a sale induced by fraud:

Provided that a notice or intimation by the vendor to the auctioneer that he intends to exercise such power in relation to any sale at the auction shall not affect the obligation of the auctioneer to deliver the goods to the purchaser.

Copy of Act to be exhibited at sale.

3. The particulars which under section seven of the Auctioneers Act, 1845, are required to be affixed or suspended in some conspicuous part of the room or place where the action is held shall include a copy of this Act, and that section shall have effect accordingly.

Appendix E

AUCTIONS (BIDDING AGREEMENTS) ACT 1969

Offences under Auctions (Bidding Agreements) Act 1927 to be indictable as well as triable summarily, and extension of time for bringing summary proceedings

1 (1) Offences under section 1 of the Auctions (Bidding Agreements) Act 1927 (which, as amended by the Criminal Justice Act 1967, renders a dealer who agrees to give, or gives, or offers a gift or consideration to another as an inducement or reward for abstaining, or for having abstained, from bidding at a sale by auction punishable on summary conviction with a fine not exceeding £400 or imprisonment for a term not exceeding six months, or both, and renders similarly punishable a person who agrees to accept, or accepts, or attempts to obtain from a dealer any such gift or consideration as aforesaid) shall be triable on indictment as well as summarily; and the penalty that may be imposed on a person on conviction on indictment of an offence under that section shall be imprisonment for a term not exceeding two years or a fine or both.

...

Persons convicted not to attend or participate in auctions

2. (1) On any such summary conviction or conviction on indictment as is mentioned in section 1 above, the court may order that the person so convicted or that person and any representative of him shall not (without leave of the court) for a period from the date of such conviction—

(a) in the case of a summary conviction, of not more than one year, or
(b) in the case of a conviction on indictment, of not more than three years,

enter upon any premises where goods intended for sale by auction are on display or to attend or participate in any way in any sale by auction.

(2) In the event of a contravention of an order under this section, the person who contravenes it (and, if he is the representative of another, that other also) shall be guilty of an offence and liable—

(a) on summary conviction, to a fine not exceeding £400;
(b) on conviction on indictment, to imprisonment for a term not exceeding two years or to a fine or to both.

(3) In any proceedings against a person in respect of a contravention of an order under this section consisting in the entry upon premises where goods intended for sale by auction were on display, it shall be a defence for him to prove that he did not know, and had no reason to suspect, that goods so intended were on display on the premises, and in any proceedings against a person in respect of a contravention of such an order consisting in his having done something as the representative of another, it shall be a defence for him to prove that he did not know, and had no reason to suspect, that that other was the subject of such an order.

(4) A person shall not be guilty of an offence under this section by reason only of his selling property by auction or causing it to be so sold.

Rights of seller of goods by auction where agreement subsists that some person shall abstain from bidding for the goods

3. (1) Where goods are purchased at an auction by a person who has entered into an agreement with another or others that the other or the others (or some of them) shall abstain from bidding for the goods (not being an agreement to purchase the goods bona fide on a joint account) and he or the other party, or one of the other parties, to the agreement is a dealer, the seller may avoid the contract under which the goods are purchased.

(2) Where a contract is avoided by virtue of the foregoing subsection, then, if the purchaser has obtained possession of the goods and restitution thereof is not made, the persons who were parties to the agreement that one or some of them should abstain from bidding for the goods the subject of the contract shall be jointly and severally liable to make good to the seller the loss (if any) he sustained by reason of the operation of the agreement.

...

(4) Section 2 of the Auctions (Bidding Agreements) Act 1927 (right of vendors to treat certain sales a fraudulent) shall not apply to a sale the contract for which is made after the commencement of the Act.

(5) In this section, 'dealer' has the meaning assigned to it by section 1(2) of the Auctions (Bidding Agreements) Action 1927.

Copy of Act to be exhibited at sale

4.   Section 3 of the Auctions (Bidding Agreements) Act 1927 (copy of Act to be exhibited at sale) shall have effect as if the reference to that Act included a reference to this Act.

References and Further Reading

Carpenter, Clive and Harris, Susan, *Property Auctions*, 1988, Estates Gazette Ltd.

Code of Measuring Practice, 4th Edition, published by RICS/ISVA.

Estates Gazette Weekly publication from Estates Gazette Ltd. Contains auction section of editorial and advertisements.

Goodie, Howard R., *Buying Bargains at Property Auctions*, 1994, Wyvern Crest, Ely.

Guidance Notes for Auctioneers proposing to sell Real Estate at Public Auction in England & Wales, published by RICS/ISVA/NAEA. New Edition 1998.

Harvey, Brian W. and Meisel, Frank, *Auctions Law and Practice,* 2nd.Edition 1995, Oxford University Press.

Learmount, Brian, *The History of the Auction*, 1985, Barnard & Learmount.

Murdoch, John, *The Law of Estate Agency and Auctions*, 3rd.Edition 1994, Estates Gazette Ltd.

Putting the Estate Agents Act 1979 and the Property Misdescriptions Act 1991 into Practice , 2nd Edition, published by RICS.

The Manual of Estate Agency Law and Practice, published by RICS. Spring 1998.

Useful published articles

CSW = Chartered Surveyor Weekly
EG = Estates Gazette

CSW. 21.03.91. 'Trial by gavel: What it takes to be a successful auctioneer'.

The Negotiator. 17.04.92. 'Under the hammer'.
CSW. 14.05.92 'ISVA slates Auctioneers over their conduct'.

CSW. 27.08.92. 'Market talk – the auction market'.

EG. 04.12.93. 'Focus '93 – Auctions', five articles.

EG. 05.02.94. 'Acting on information provided'.
CSM. March 1994. 'Banging the gavel'.

The Valuer. July 1994. 'Do exemption clauses work?'.

EG. 03.12.94. 'Focus '94 – Auctions', five articles.

EG. 28.01.95. 'Misdescription: Vendors beware'.

EG. 13.05.95. 'A fair test? Unfair contract terms and auctions'.

EG. 19.08.95. 'Ground rules for ground rents'.

EG. 26.08.95. 'Is a nod as good as a wink?'.

EG. 02.09.95. 'Truth, half truths and the law'.

The Valuer. November 1995. 'Honesty is the best policy'.

EG. 09.12.95. 'Focus '95 – Auctions', four articles.

EG. 13.01.96. 'Landlord and Tenant Act and auctions'.

EG. 20.01.96. '1996: a new chapter for auctions'.

EG. 03.02.96. 'Full house for residential sales'.

EG. 07.12.96. 'Focus '96 – Auctions', five articles'

EG. 25.01.97. 'Televised auctions could soon hit the right note'.

EG. 09.08.97. 'Auctions take a leading role'.

EG. 16.08.97. 'Act anomaly slammed'. (Housing Act 1996)

EG. 30.08.97. 'Getting in on the Act – The Housing Act 1996'.

The Valuer. 09/10.97. 'A barrister's cautionary tale: Bidding on behalf of vendor by the auctioneer and by the vendor – pitfalls'.

CSM. October 1997 A similar report to the above.

EG. 13.12.97. Auction Report: 'New Guidance Notes for Property Auctioneers –
a preview of moves afoot on clarifying Conditions'.

EG. 20.12.97. First catalogue on the Internet.

EG. 17.01.98. 'Faxwise keeps buyers ahead'.

EG. 24.01.98. 'ARAS reveals bumper totals'.

EG. 21.02.98. 'Worth banging on about'.

Index